# Cross-curricular Primary Practice

# Cross-curricular Primary Practice:
## Taking a Leadership Role

*Edited by*

Rosemary Webb

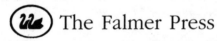 The Falmer Press

(A member of the Taylor & Francis Group)
London • Washington, D.C.

**UK**      Falmer Press, 1 Gunpowder Square, London, EC4A 3DE

**USA**    Falmer Press, Taylor & Francis Inc., 1900 Frost Road, Suite 101, Bristol, PA 19007

---

First published in 1996

**A catalogue record for this book is available from the British Library**

ISBN 0 7507 0491 8 cased
ISBN 0 7507 0492 6 paper

**Library of Congress Cataloging-in-Publication Data are available on request**

Jacket design by Caroline Archer

Typeset in 10/12 pt Garamond by
Graphicraft Typesetters Ltd., Hong Kong.

*Printed in Great Britain by Biddles Ltd., Guildford and King's Lynn on paper which has a specified pH value on final paper manufacture of not less than 7.5 and is therefore 'acid free'.*

# Contents

# Introduction

*Rosemary Webb*

> Attainment targets and programmes of study are the bricks with which the new curriculum must be built. Cross curricular strategies bond these bricks into a cohesive structure. (NCC, 1989, para.19)

The view taken in this book is that cross-curricular practice is an integral part of what is needed to meet National Curriculum requirements and to give these requirements an overall coherence. Furthermore, cross-curricular practice provides rich opportunities to work with children to develop the knowledge, skills and concepts that they will need to cope with, and to enjoy, the complexities and the challenges of the twenty-first century. Thus it serves to compensate for the limitations of the National Curriculum which has been criticized for being overly orientated to the past and for being incomplete (see, for example, Alexander, 1993). It can also greatly enhance the whole curriculum through making a 'virtue of cultural diversity while challenging prejudice in all its forms including racism, sexism and ethnocentrism in particular' (Verma, 1994, p.15).

It is also timely to focus attention on cross-curricular practice. The revision of the National Curriculum to reduce the acknowledged content overload (Dearing, 1993) and to aid the simplification of the assessment requirements opens up the possibility of teaching time being devoted to areas other than those specified in the Orders. School staffs, who are engaging in a process of reviewing policies and plans in the light of the new National Curriculum Orders, have the opportunity to ensure that these are informed by those areas of interest and issues of concern particular to their schools, which have been put to one side in order to cope with the demands of the Education Reform Act (1988) and subsequent legislation. The message that 'the way in which teaching is timetabled and how lessons are described and organised cannot be prescribed' (DES, 1989, para.4.3) has constantly been reiterated. However, belief in this message has been severely tested in the face of political and media attention, which has often been derisive of primary education, the pressures of preparing for, and responding to, the findings of OFSTED inspections and most recently OFSTED's criticisms of unsatisfactory standards of achievement in reading, writing and numeracy (OFSTED, 1995). Nevertheless, in many

*1*

primary schools, there is a renewed determination, often underpinned by cautious optimism about the future, that they are going to take greater control over the ways in which the National Curriculum is interpreted and taught in their schools. This is irrespective of whether or not the notional 20 per cent of curriculum time, supposedly freed up by the revisions to the Orders, materializes or whether, owing to the uncertain political climate, the promised moratorium on curriculum change manages to be sustained for five years.

This book provides a discussion of the theory and practice of important aspects of cross-curricular practice and considers how such practice might be coordinated and developed across the school. In putting together the collection, a decision had to be made as to whether to adopt a broad brush approach over a wide range of practice or to be selective and therefore able to discuss the aspects chosen in greater depth. We decided that we would adopt the latter approach and the reasons for our choice of chapter topics are given below. However, we appreciate that this means we have omitted aspects of cross-curricular practice for which readers could make equally sound justifications for inclusion. For primary schools interested in reviewing all aspects of cross-curricular practice, or others in addition to those presented here, they might use this book in combination with related works, such as Verma and Pumfrey (1994) and Siraj-Blatchford and Siraj-Blatchford (1995).

NCC (1990) distinguishes three aspects of cross-curricular provision: dimensions, skills and themes. These distinctions are helpful when reflecting on, organizing and planning cross-curricular practice. They also serve to differentiate cross-curricular provision, especially themes, from the use of topic work. Topic is generally understood to be a form of curriculum organization, often enquiry-based, which integrates aspects of different National Curriculum subjects. Research five years after the introduction of the National Curriculum indicates topic is still the dominant form of curriculum organization in primary schools, albeit with changes taking place to a more subject-focused variety of topic, especially at Key Stage 2 (Webb and Vulliamy, 1996).

Cross-curricular dimensions 'are concerned with the intentional promotion of personal and social development through the curriculum as a whole' (NCC, 1989, p.2). They may be addressed within specific lessons or events, such as assemblies, but should permeate all of the curriculum and areas of school life. Major cross-curricular dimensions include equal opportunities and multicultural education. We have chosen to focus on improving the learning experiences of pupils with special educational needs because of the importance we attach to this and because schools are currently reviewing their provision in the light of the Code of Practice (1994). We have included discipline as an additional dimension. Discipline is another topical subject given the pressures to create classroom conditions conducive to covering content and high attainment, owing to the demands of the National Curriculum and testing in the context of open enrolment and the associated rise in exclusion rates. While the involvement and influence of parents does not readily fit within NCC's descriptions of cross-curricular dimensions, it certainly increasingly pervades and influences many aspects of primary school life and affects not only the personal and social but also the intellectual development of children. For this reason we felt it should be represented within this collection.

Cross-curricular skills are exceedingly numerous and are often grouped together under umbrella terms — for example, communication skills can be viewed as encompassing listening skills, oracy and literacy. For bilingual pupils, developing their communication skills in English is vital to enable them to participate fully and derive maximum benefit from their schooling. Hence the inclusion of advice for teachers in teaching English as a second language was regarded as essential. Pupil self-assessment is increasingly being incorporated in schools' assessment practices as part of records of achievement and to contribute to teacher assessment. The chapter on this provides an opportunity to consider how pupils may be helped to develop the skills involved.

NCC describes the cross-curricular themes as those 'elements which enrich the educational experience of pupils' (1989, p.3) and the five that they choose to address in their curriculum guidance are:

- economic and industrial understanding;
- careers education and guidance;
- environmental education;
- health education; and
- citizenship.

We have included a chapter on environmental education because, although it has taken various forms from nature study to broad-based topics on such issues as conservation, since the 1960s it has been a valued part of the primary curriculum and is one that readily excites and motivates our increasingly environmentally conscious youngsters. The move to more subject-focused work, especially at Key Stage 2, the implementation of the revised Orders in August 1995 and the long- and medium-term planning currently being undertaken in response to this makes it timely to review the contribution of this theme to the curriculum and to create new opportunities for its study. Global education is a theme which acknowledges that the problems and challenges that this and future generations will face are a product of complex interrelationships on a global scale and seeks through content and classroom processes to develop children's awareness of these global connections and their location within them. While seldom using the term education for citizenship, primary schools — especially, perhaps, small schools — view this as an important part of their role. However, this theme has been conveyed to pupils through the ethos of the school and the daily routines, responsibilities and relationships which contribute to this. Given the changing social and political climate, which for many children may have a confusing, demoralizing or turbulent effect on their lives, it may be time to review the messages transmitted in this way, consider if these need modifying, or adding to, and whether through particular actions, events or lessons some should be made more explicit and openly discussed.

We have added media education to the themes because of its increasing impact on, and contribution to, our lives. We feel it deserves to be removed from 'the margins' and given greater emphasis because of its increasing centrality to children's lives and the ongoing debate on the effect on them of television and videos and the material accessed by computers. Children need to be able to cope with, to discuss and to critically reflect upon that which they have experienced.

Attempts to promote more teaching and learning of cross-curricular themes, such as those referred to above, have often been bedevilled by their lower status in relation to the more traditional academic subjects. Thus, for example, one of the key aspects of Dore's (1976) influential 'diploma disease' thesis is that, since in all societies schooling acts as a vital selective mechanism via certification, what is taught in the classroom is severely constrained by the strictures of examination syllabi in the high status subjects. In developing countries, especially, this has acted as a major constraint, as Vulliamy's (1987) discussion of the difficulties of implementing environmental education illustrates. However, such constraints have also been seen to operate at secondary level in this country where the traditionally high status academic subjects tend to take precedence at GCSE and A levels. Many educationalists have viewed the introduction of the National Curriculum as likely to exacerbate such biasses against cross-curricular work — Hargreaves, for example, arguing that:

> Academic subjects are in the ascendant. Little time, status or importance is to be given to aesthetic, practical or social and personal subjects, still less to forms of learning that have no clear subject designation at all. In the small portion of the curriculum remaining after the core and foundation subjects have been accounted for, there will be little time or space for social and personal education, political education, environmental education, development education, integrated studies, social studies, peace studies and the like. (Hargreaves, 1989, p.64)

There are a number of reasons, however, why English primary schools should represent something of an exception to this downgrading in status of cross-curricular work. Firstly, primary school teachers have for many years, following the influence of the Plowden Report, organized the curriculum on a thematic topic-based structure. Secondly, primary school teachers, again reflecting the influence of Plowden, tend to have a strong commitment to child-centred experiential forms of teaching and learning. Thirdly, since the abolition of the 11-plus, English primary schools have been relatively insulated from the examination backwash effects of the certification system associated with the diploma disease. Whether compulory national testing at ages 7 and 11 years in the three core subjects, linked with the publication of school results in league tables, will bring about stronger pressures to concentrate especially on the core subjects remains to be seen. However, just as research indicates that primary teachers' core values have to date led to the maintenance of topic work and experiential teaching styles despite the introduction of the National Curriculum (Vulliamy and Webb, 1993; Webb and Vulliamy, 1996), it seems likely that teachers' commitments to cross-curricular practice will also be maintained.

Interestingly, Duncan Graham, the first Chief Executive of the National Curriculum Council, recounts how one of his major battles with civil servants in the Education Department concerned their decision that the NCC should not proceed with the publication of its guidance on the five cross-curricular themes — a decision which was reversed only after a private meeting between Graham and Kenneth Baker, the Secretary of State for Education (Graham and Tytler, 1993, pp.19–22). Recognizing that teachers themselves placed a high priority on cross-curricular work, Graham concluded that:

> The five documents on the cross-curricular themes of citizenship, health, the environment, industrial and economic understanding and careers were the most obvious example of ministerial panic and interference. John MacGregor in particular had been impressed with the argument from the independent schools that they would undermine standards as they would deflect from the main curriculum. This was a complete misunderstanding of their purpose. Teachers would want to enter these areas and the booklets were intended to guide them in ways which enhance the curriculum not detract from it. (Graham and Tytler, 1993, p.105)

This book is aimed particularly at teachers in training and newly qualified teachers who wish to extend their understanding of cross-curricular practice and who are inexperienced in taking the lead or coordinating an area of work. However, there are also useful suggestions for experienced teachers, who may be relatively unfamiliar with the less established themes discussed here — such as media education and global education — or are encountering for the first time areas in which they have received little or no training, such as the development of English as a second language. These chapters may also provide a helpful starting point for review by a working party or the whole staff of the issues that they address.

Chapter 1 considers the implications of the Code of Practice and the revised National Curriculum for meeting children's special educational needs in the classroom. It looks particularly at the effect on children's motivation and success in learning of the classroom environment and the ways in which tasks are presented. The special educational needs coordinator, whose responsibilities have been considerably expanded by the Code, is shown to have a vital role in providing ideas and support for classteachers.

The focus on the quality of the classroom environment and how it affects children's learning and self-esteem is continued in Chapter 2 by Pamela Munn. She draws on the findings of research to provide a way of thinking about classroom discipline to enable teachers to analyse their practice and better understand why some activities go well while others are unsuccessful. The impact on behaviour of three key interrelated features are discussed: teachers' actions, the classroom context and the teacher's goals. Through practical suggestions she encourages teachers to identify factors in a positive classroom situation where there are few if any discipline problems. Contrasting these with factors identified in a situation where pupils' behaviour is troublesome reveals ways in which these key features of classroom life might be modified to promote improved behaviour.

In Chapter 3 Hilary Emery considers the ways in which pupils might be more fully involved in the purpose of classroom activities and the planning of their learning through participating in the evaluation of their work. She argues that this process can develop children's self-esteem and lead them to identify their strengths and maximize their successes. She acknowledges the demands on teacher time and classroom management that accompanies initiating and maintaining pupil self-assessment. However, she suggests that these can be minimized through working with children to set clear achievable learning targets, peer review, the involvement of parents and the use of self-assessment sheets.

In Chapter 4 Lynne Cameron focuses on the multilingual classroom which places fundamental demands on teachers to seek simultaneously to make the curriculum content accessible and interesting to children and to use it as a vehicle to develop their English language skills. She argues that not only is it vital for the children's future lives and careers that teachers strive to improve their teaching of these skills, but also that in doing so teachers' own cultural horizons are broadened and they come to a deeper knowledge of how language is structured by, and structures, our understanding of the world. She opens her chapter by briefly reviewing provision in Britain from an international perspective and the issues this raises. She then turns to research to identify some key principles for guiding English language development across the curriculum. Finally, she suggests ideas to help class teachers and language coordinators to plan and implement activities which challenge the thinking and develop the English language skills of bilingual children.

In the fifth chapter in the collection Margot Brown considers how the principles and practice of global education can deepen children's knowledge of people and places in the world and their impact on our everyday lives and in doing so render children able to challenge any negative and erroneous stereotypes that they might encounter. She argues that through learning about people and communities in localities different from our own, children can develop a deeper understanding of their own community and themselves. For proponents of global education the learning process is of equal importance to the content of learning. Hence the teaching methods used, which foster active learning through cooperative endeavour, investigation, problem-solving and discussion, serve to reinforce the underlying principles of equal opportunities, self-awareness, empowerment and interdependence. She shows how these ideas can be translated into practice within the context of teaching the National Curriculum by looking in detail at an inner city primary school project.

In common with global education and citizenship, environmental education also aims to encourage children to explore and understand the world and its peoples in order to engage in informed debate, to make decisions and to take actions which aim to maintain and improve the quality of human life. In Chapter 6, in her advice on ways of including environmental education in the primary school curriculum, Joy Palmer shows how the National Curriculum provides a framework for including many important aspects of this theme. She examines the knowledge, concepts, skills and attitudes commonly agreed to be fundamental to environmental education, prior to identifying opportunities for planning and timetabling work which incorporates these. The guidelines she provides for building up a range of up-to-date resources for use with their classes will be helpful for teachers seeking ideas about how to procure information and materials on all themes.

Chapter 7 by Ian Davies argues that education for citizenship should be included in the primary curriculum. However, he considers it crucial that teachers are clear about the rationale underpinning the particular stance on citizenship they adopt and the kinds of activities in which they involve their pupils. To assist in this he looks at developments in citizenship and the values underpinning them and offers a critique of the National Curriculum Council's (1990) guidance on citizenship education and the report and recommendations of the Speaker's Commission on Citizenship (1990). His position is that citizenship education should be geared towards creating a situation whereby young people are taking part in setting their own agendas and contributing constructively and critically to an enriched democratic society. He concludes by showing how this might be embarked upon in the primary school.

Media education is the subject of Chapter 8. Ken Fox argues that the popular media are important in children's culture and the knowledge of this that they bring to school may be harnessed by teachers to promote their self-image and contribute to their learning. He provides a description of media education and three frameworks to use as a starting point for examining media products and the audiences and intentions to which they are geared. He stresses the importance of encouraging pupils to ask questions about the meanings and implications of these products in order to promote critical thinking about the media and its role in their lives. In his suggestions for practical activities on image analysis and awareness of place he demonstrates that lack of resources and technological knowledge need not inhibit teachers from getting started. Many materials — such as photographs, magazine pictures, birthday cards — which are readily available can provide stimulus for media work in a range of curricular contexts.

In Chapter 9 John Bastiani provides an analysis of the development of schools' work with parents in the context of the current market ideology, the growing experience of parental involvement in all aspects of their children's schooling and government cuts in education budgets, which have reduced the staffing for home–school initiatives. He argues that at this stage in the evolution of home–school work the dominant metaphor of 'partnership' for this work is unhelpful and unrepresentative of what is actually happening. Following consideration of the impact of contemporary conditions and pressures on schools' relationship with parents, he sets out an agenda for a whole-school approach to working with parents which takes these into account and is based on recognized 'good practice' in this area. He ends by being cautiously optimistic that future developments will be successful and have substantial positive effects, providing that in their reviews of policies and practices, schools are willing to consult, involve and listen to the diverse opinions of the parents themselves.

Taking the lead in reviewing, coordinating and developing cross-curricular practice is the subject of the concluding Chapter 10 by Graham Vulliamy and myself. We begin by considering what leadership in the context of cross-curricular practice might mean and identify factors which could constrain or promote development work. Collecting evidence upon which to base decisions and move forward is viewed as vital and so we discuss strategies for doing this: carrying out 'audits'; working with critical friends; and embarking on small-scale action-research enquiries. Disseminating information to colleagues also forms a fundamental strategy in any initiative and so we discuss the organization of meetings and INSET. We conclude by emphasizing the need to gain the support of colleagues if individual enthusiasms are to be converted into practice across the school.

## References

ALEXANDER, R. (1993) 'Innocence and experience: Reconstructing primary education', Inaugural lecture, 13 December, University of Leeds.

DEARING, R. (1993) *The National Curriculum and its Assessment, Final Report*, London, SCAA.

DEPARTMENT OF EDUCATION AND SCIENCE (1989) *National Curriculum From Policy to Practice*, London, DES.

DORE, R. (1976) *The Diploma Disease*, London, Allen and Unwin.

GRAHAM, D. and TYTLER, D. (1993) *A Lesson for Us All: The Makings of the National Curriculum*, London, Routledge.

HARGREAVES, A. (1989) *Curriculum and Assessment Reform*, Milton Keynes, Open University Press.

NATIONAL CURRICULUM COUNCIL (1989) *The National Curriculum and Whole Curriculum Planning: Preliminary Guidance, Circular Number 6*, York, NCC.

NATIONAL CURRICULUM COUNCIL (1990) *The Whole Curriculum, Curriculum Guidance 3*, York, NCC.

OFSTED (1995) *The Annual Report of Her Majesty's Chief Inspector for Schools*, London, HMSO.

SIRAJ-BLATCHFORD, J. and SIRAJ-BLATCHFORD, I. (Eds) (1995) *Educating the Whole Child: Cross-curricular Skills, Themes and Dimensions*, Buckingham, Open University Press.

SPEAKER'S COMMISSION ON CITIZENSHIP (1990) *Encouraging Citizenship*, London, HMSO.

VERMA, G.K. (1994) 'Cultural diversity in primary schools: Its nature, extent and cross-curricular implications', in VERMA, G.V. and PUMFREY, P.D. (Eds) (1994) *Cross-*

*curricular Contexts, Themes and Dimensions in the Primary school: Volume 4 Cultural Diversity and the Curriculum*, London, Falmer Press.

VERMA, G.V. and PUMFREY, P.D. (Eds) (1994) *Cross-curricular Contexts, Themes and Dimensions in the Primary School: Volume 4 Cultural Diversity and the Curriculum*, London, Falmer Press.

VULLIAMY, G. (1987) 'Environmental education in Third World schools: Rhetoric or realism?', *The Environmentalist*, **7**, pp.11–19.

VULLIAMY, G. and WEBB, R. (1993) 'Progressive education and the National Curriculum: Findings from a global education research project', *Educational Review*, **45**, 1, pp.21–41.

WEBB, R. and VULLIAMY, G. (1996) *Roles and Responsibilities in the Primary School: Changing Demands, Changing Practices*, Buckingham, Open University Press.

# Chapter 1

# Meeting Special Educational Needs in the Classroom

*Rosemary Webb*

The Education Act (1993), which introduced the Code of Practice governing the identification and assessment of all special educational needs (SEN), is part of a series of legislation set in motion by the 1988 Education Reform Act (ERA). This has led to a situation where schools are immersed in the implementation of multiple innovations which in combination make enormous demands for change in school policies and practices. This chapter examines the curriculum and classroom provision for children with special educational needs, especially those without statements, in the context of some of these demands. It considers how aspects of the classroom environment and the differentiation of tasks and activities can improve their learning experiences. It also examines the role of the Special Educational Needs Coordinator (SENCO) who plays a vital part not only in establishing the quality and range of this provision but also in generating the interest and commitment of class teachers to maintain and develop it.

In discussing issues and offering advice in relation to the implementation of the National Curriculum and children with SEN, I shall draw particularly on two phases of qualitative research sponsored by the Association of Teachers and Lecturers (ATL) which were carried out in fifty primary schools across thirteen LEAs between October 1992 and February 1994. The first phase focused on the implementation of the National Curriculum at Key Stage 2 and the second on the changing roles and responsibilities of primary school teachers (Webb and Vulliamy, 1996).

### The Code of Practice

The 1994 Code of Practice (DfE, 1994) required by the 1993 Education Act was introduced to ensure better provision for both the 2 per cent of pupils who need statements and the notional 18 per cent with SEN who are not statemented. The definition of SEN remains the same as that given in the Education Act 1981. Thus 'a child has special educational needs if he or she has a learning difficulty which calls for special educational provision to be made for him or her' (section 156). The Code, which sets out the respective duties of schools and education authorities in providing for these pupils and gives detailed principles and procedures to be followed, aims to address the issues raised in two reports by the Audit Commission (1992a and 1992b) which identified major inconsistencies between LEAs and schools in SEN practices and policies throughout England and Wales. These procedures are set within the framework of responsibilities of a school's governing body to provide for pupils with SEN and to publish details of this provision at the school's annual meeting, in the school's annual report and in summary form in the school prospectus. The Code is a non-statutory document. However, those to whom it applies have a statutory duty 'to have regard to it' and the regulations to which it refers are statutory. As explored by Garner (1995), there is considerable potential for tension between the Code's guidance and the statutory regulations. However, during OFSTED inspections schools will need to demonstrate how the Code is being interpreted and implemented.

Lewis (1995) describes the findings of a questionnaire survey designed to collect information about primary schools' special needs policies and provision in order to better understand how equipped they were to implement the Code. The survey was published in Junior Education (April 1994) and 292 primary schools elected to respond. The majority of schools (87.2 per cent) reported having written a SEN policy document and most of these were produced within the three years leading up to the survey. Lewis (1995) found that 'the plurality and variation of personnel, timetabling arrangements, and tasks of the SENCO were striking' (p.14). In 11 per cent of schools the head was responsible for SEN and in 252 schools (86 per cent) there was a SENCO who was someone other than the headteacher. Only about one third (38.4 per cent) had an incentive allowance specifically for SEN. Approximately two-thirds of SENCOs also held other responsibilities as well as class teaching and in about one quarter of the schools the role was filled by someone with significant additional managerial responsibilities. In twelve schools (4.8 per cent) the role was filled by a part-time teacher. She found that:

> In the vast majority of schools with a SENCO any one special educational needs related activity occupied less than 2 hours per week. The general picture was of a highly fragmented and diversified role. (Lewis, 1995, p.17)

## Special Educational Needs Coordinators

Every school must now appoint a special educational needs coordinator (SENCO). While this role is central to the implementation of the Code, in the majority of primary schools it has not been created by it. The introduction of the 1981 Education Act based on the recommendations of the Warnock Report led to a steady increase in the designation of posts of responsibility for SEN.

However, as Moss (1994) comments: 'In some schools this developed into no more than a relatively perfunctory function; in others it was a senior appointment with the post holder already doing as much, if not more, than the Code recommends' (p.1).

The impact of the Code of Practice on the role of SEN coordinators is massive. It states that they should be responsible for:

- the day-to-day operation of the school's SEN policy;
- liaising with and advising fellow teachers;
- coordinating provision for children with special educational needs;
- maintaining the school's SEN register and overseeing the records on all pupils with special educational needs;
- liaising with parents of children with special educational needs;
- contributing to the in-service training of staff; and
- liaising with external agencies, including the educational psychology service and other support agencies, medical and social services and voluntary bodies. (para.2:14)

During the first three of the five stages in the identification and assessment of SEN set out in the Code, SEN identification, provision and monitoring are based in schools — although advice and support may be sought from external specialists. During stages 3 and 4 the local authority shares responsibility with schools. SENCOs have a vital part to play in administering the first three of the five stages — especially stage 2 when the SENCO takes the lead in managing provision. A further dimension is also given to the role of many coordinators in relation to the drafting of individual education plans (IEPs), the new procedures for the annual review of statements (the organization of which the headteacher may delegate to the SENCO), and the introduction in the 1993 Education Act of SEN tribunals which will be held regionally to hear appeals. The introduction of the tribunals raises the possibility of schools and teachers who have not had 'regard' to the Code being found negligent, which places additional pressure on SENCOs to maintain thorough and accurate records of children's needs and to develop the provision made to meet those needs.

Lewis (1995) found that most SENCOs have little non-contact time to carry out their role and approximately one-third of teachers with this responsibility had no non-contact time. Where a school had some non-contact time for SENCOs to carry out SEN work, the most popular use of that time was for withdrawal group work followed by — but a long way behind — in-class support for colleagues. Lack of non-contact time seriously undermines the efficiency of SENCOs. The paperwork alone, which is required by the Code, is enormously time-consuming. For example, the SEN register needs to be updated regularly and additions to children's records need to be made following consultations with specialists, meetings with parents and actions taken by staff. Gains (1994) outlined eight major functions for the SENCO under the Code only one of which directly involved them with the process of teaching and learning. This leads Garner (1995) to suggest that perhaps 'the Code of practice is simply bureaucratising a group of experienced SEN teachers, effectively reducing the amount of time they spend with their pupils' (p.6).

All schools are now required to have a special educational needs policy which had to be published by 1 August 1995. This must include information on the school's special educational provision, the identification and assessment of pupils with SEN, relevant in-service training, external links and cooperation with parents and the criteria for evaluating the success of the policy. While this policy is the overall responsibility of the headteacher and governors it is likely that the SENCO will take the lead in working with staff to produce it. As with the drafting of curriculum policies (Webb, 1994), a range of approaches was being taken to get these into place as speedily as possible. Some SENCOs either revised existing policies, or drafted new ones, by themselves in consultation with the head, senior management team and in some cases the SEN governor. Alternatively, policies were the focus of school professional development days where staff brainstormed ideas and these were converted into a policy document by the SENCO or a working party. Then this was circulated for comment or became the subject of a staff meeting called to obtain feedback. By this process of negotiation a document was ultimately decided upon. There was general agreement that the greater the staff involvement in producing the policy the more commitment there would be to its implementation.

Implementing the first stage of the Code appears to be causing the most difficulties. This places responsibility on the class teacher to identify a child's SEN, gather information — ranging from evidence of National Curriculum attainment and standardized test results to observations of behaviour — and to take initial action to meet those needs. Arrangements also need to be made for monitoring the child's progress and for a review of the provision put into place. As argued by Visser (1994), placing the responsibility for SEN on the class teacher has positive implications:

> It avoids the de-skilling process which can all too easily become part of special educational provision. There remains a tendency in special education for teachers to believe that the SENCO has all the answers in meeting the needs of the pupil with SEN. . . . The Code encourages cooperation between staff in meeting special educational needs. . .(Visser, 1994, p.27)

However, class teachers will need different degrees of support in fulfilling their responsibilities. For some systematizing their existing practice will be sufficient while others will need considerable support and practical advice. Many teachers do not have the training or experience required to recognize the wide range of different types of learning difficulty which might be experienced by some of the children in their classes. This could lead to the source of these children's difficulties going unrecognized. Therefore the guidance that

SENCOs can provide for their colleagues is vital. This is likely to take the form of the provision of resources describing and targetting particular types of need (for example, Webster *et al.*, 1994), information on sources of external help, advice on the collection of appropriate evidence, strategies and resources to help children's learning and assistance with the preparation of IEPs and the writing of reports.

As identified by Buchanan (1995), in the context of heavy workloads caused by the implementation of the National Curriculum and its associated assessments class teachers under pressure might be reluctant to identify the existence of pupils with SEN in their classes because doing so generates additional paperwork, assessment and communications with parents. In schools, where — as perhaps is too frequently the case — SENCOs have responsibility without power, this potential conflict of interest between the SENCO and the classteacher needs recognizing and addressing. While personalities influence the way in which such situations are handled and good interpersonal skills and leadership qualities on the part of the SENCO are important, a supportive management structure must be put in place in order that tasks may be delegated and carried out and conflicts, whether between parents, children or colleagues, can be avoided or at least resolved swiftly. As found by Webb (1994), where responsibility for SEN is shared by the head and the SENCO this gives more clout to decision-making. However, if aspects of the shared role are not carefully delineated, this can lead to resentment, overlapping work and time wasted.

Some schools (see for example, Harvey, 1995) find it useful to have termly year group or key stage meetings — depending on the size of the school — in order to review the progress and the strategies being used to help children with SEN. These are attended by the head, deputy or other members of the senior management team, the class teachers concerned and others who may work with the children being discussed, such as teachers' aides and the home–school liaison teacher. External experts, such as the educational psychologist, may also attend meetings where their advice would be particularly useful. To make the meetings as effective as possible the SENCO draws up an agenda, gathers evidence to support the discussions, takes minutes to record the decisions made and action points agreed and communicates these in writing to those concerned.

While meetings, such as these, add to the administrative load of SENCOs, they also provide them with support. Especially where SENCOs have little non-contact time, it is vital that aspects of the role can be shared. Hence, the school secretary might assist with the administration, a home–school liaison teacher might communicate information on children's progress to parents and feed back concerns, a teacher's aide might assist in the preparation of teaching materials, the head might take responsibility for liaison with outside agencies and the INSET coordinator could help arrange training opportunities. Implementing the SEN policy is a whole school responsibility, which is likely to be tackled with greater thoroughness, if everyone makes a contribution. A team approach is also necessary to make the role manageable for the SENCO. As one primary school SENCO put it:

> The SEN co-ordinator has a responsibility to her/himself. There is going to be a great deal of work involved in implementing the Code, and this will place demands on the time of the SEN co-ordinator. It will be hard, but it is important to keep things in perspective and try to plan change and development so that they can be implemented in a manageable and realistic way, and so that the role of SEN co-ordinator is rewarding rather than impossible. (Harvey, 1995, p.82)

### Impact of the National Curriculum

*individual's legal right*

The principle of the entitlement for all pupils to share the same statutory right to the National Curriculum was broadly welcomed when the National Curriculum was introduced. However, making this a real possibility is often a very complex and demanding process. Research into the implementation of the National Curriculum at Key Stage 2 (Webb, 1993) revealed that in some schools the additional work required to draw up plans and policies for the implementation of the National Curriculum meant that producing or reviewing the school's SEN policy was 'put on the back burner'. However, in other schools the implementation of the National Curriculum caused them to rethink their approach to SEN support in order to protect pupils' entitlement. Thus, one junior school decided that instead of withdrawing pupils for extra help with 'the basics' they would use the withdrawal time to do practical activities in mathematics and science to develop the skills of investigation, problem-solving and cooperation with others. Most of the pupils with SEN found these activities very demanding and sometimes upsetting and those with emotional and behavioural difficulties could not readily work with their peers. In a supportive closely supervised environment, where individual assistance was immediately available, the children could be helped to overcome their difficulties.

Overwhelmingly in schools in the ATL research, teachers considered that curriculum overload caused inadequate time to be spent on basic numeracy and literacy, especially listening to pupils reading, and led to work being 'rushed' or skimmed over' resulting in it being unfinished or of poor quality. The pace and volume of work to be got through was thought to be particularly stressful for pupils with SEN who were 'just swamped by it'. They tended to be the children with the most unfinished work, as there were fewer opportunities for them to be given the extra time needed to complete it. This meant that their opportunities to experience success were reduced considerably. Also, if a choice of activities was given to those who had finished, they seldom had the chance to participate.

Hopefully a slimmed down National Curriculum will enable teachers to recover some of the time that they feel has been lost for getting to know their pupils, interacting with them and taking account of their particular interests and aptitudes. Also fewer knowledge requirements and the possibility of teaching aspects of the programmes of study either in depth or in outline should remove some of the pressure that teachers have been under 'to push pupils through the National Curriculum'. Providing the notional 20 per cent of time freed up for discretionary use becomes a reality, this could be used to allow pupils more time to complete tasks, exercise choice over activities, address areas of weakness and work to their strengths. However, as argued by Campbell (1994), given that the time allocations in the Dearing Report for English and mathematics are dramatically lower than current practice and that traditionally the basics have been a predominant concern for primary schools, which is likely to be reinforced further by the demands of testing, any additional time created is likely to be spent on these. Consequently, teachers of pupils with SEN will particularly need to guard against an overemphasis on the basics at the expense of pupil enjoyment and development in other curriculum areas.

Stevens (1994) describes how the process of revising the National Curriculum Orders addressed the issues identified in the Dearing review (Dearing, 1993) relating to pupils with a wide range of SEN. Specialists in SEN from both mainstream and special schools were included on the key stage and subject advisory groups and a set of SEN principles was drawn up to provide a framework against which to consider the groups' proposals as they emerged. Peter (1995) considers that there is a helpful consistency between the revised National Curriculum Orders and the Code of Practice which 'shows itself in at least three ways: curricular access, differentiation and the voice of the child' (p.35). By aiming to identify and address difficulties early in a child's schooling, the Code seeks to increase the possibility of access to the whole curriculum including the National Curriculum for pupils with SEN. Prior to the revision of the Orders pupils were required to work within the programmes of study for their key stage. Now enabling statements make it clear that they may work at whichever level of the National Curriculum is most appropriate without the need for a statement of SEN or the modification of an existing one. In addition, access statements, which introduce each new subject Order, stress the need for appropriate support for pupils with communication, sensory or physical difficulties to help ensure that they can be provided with sufficiently challenging work.

Perhaps, surprisingly the access statements do not include any reference to pupils with emotional and behavioural difficulties. The implementation of the National Curriculum has caused teachers to be particularly concerned about pupils with such problems both in relation to their own motivation and progress and, if their difficulties result in disruptive behaviour, the effect that they can have in upsetting a class and constraining the progress of their peers. Some schools have reviewed their discipline policies in order: to establish among staff shared positive expectations of standards of pupil behaviour; to promote a consistent approach to sanctions and rewards; to set up procedures for contacting the parents of disruptive pupils; and to initiate home–school liaison over action for improving their behaviour. The rise in the number of exclusions at primary level demonstrates the need for a whole school approach to develop and implement positive strategies for helping such pupils. The role of the SENCO in relation to school discipline and exclusions will be largely determined by whether behavioural difficulties are viewed as part of the school's pastoral responsibilities, which have traditionally been overseen by the head or deputy, or as an aspect of SEN. In schools where pastoral concerns are a major area of work, while the input of the SENCO on discipline and exclusion matters will be very important, including overall responsibility for these within the SENCOs role would make it unmanageably broad in scope.

In addition to requiring criteria by which to assess and plan for progression for all pupils, stage 1 of the Code and the IEPs for children with SEN at stages 2 and 3 require detailed information on National Curriculum assessment and the objectives to be achieved. The research into the implementation of the National Curriculum at Key Stage 2 (Webb, 1993) showed that teachers found the statements of attainment in the original Orders useful as a framework for progression and as objectives around which to devise activities and assessment tasks. Now planning is based on the programmes of study, these props have been removed and teachers are expected to devise their own learning objectives. In a school, in which I am currently researching, as interim measures in the formulation of objectives teachers are both matching the old statements of attainment to the new programmes of study and breaking down the programmes of study into discrete statements. This is clearly an area requiring whole school discussion and the provision of guidance at local and national level. In order to provide a basis for such guidance, the SCAA has commissioned the National Foundation for Educational Research to carry out research into effective practice that schools are using currently to assess, record and report the progress of pupils with SEN including those working at levels 1, 2 or 3 for several years or within more than one key stage (Stevens, 1995).

### Classroom Environment

The environment of the school as a whole and the classroom in particular will influence greatly children's enjoyment of, and progress in, the National Curriculum and other activities. The classroom needs to be both a secure base and a source of stimuli for learning. A national working group considering the implications of the introduction of the National Curriculum for pupils with SEN drew up a checklist of factors contributing to a positive learning environment (NCC, 1989). The group emphasized that pupils with SEN are likely to have even stronger needs than other pupils for 'a climate of warmth and support in which self-confidence and self-esteem can grow and in which all pupils feel valued and able to risk making mistakes as they learn, without fear of criticism' (p.8).

Teachers are urged to apply the notion of 'fitness for purpose' to select the most suitable teaching methods and resources to meet the learning objectives planned for all children (Alexander *et al.*, 1992). While, on the one hand, more whole class teaching may be occuring, especially at Key Stage 2, as a result of rising class sizes, the content demands of the National Curriculum and exhortations to make greater use of this form of classroom organization, the importance of speaking and listening, investigating and problem solving across the Orders have encouraged teachers to extend their range of methods. This is very important because, as research into learning styles suggests, pupils have preferred learning styles (Pike and Selby, 1988) and need to experience a range of teaching approaches to increase their opportunities for learning and to enable them to become aware of the ways in which they learn most readily. However, whatever teaching approaches are used, a clear message coming through classroom research over the last twenty years is that a major factor in improving pupils' learning is experiencing sustained higher-order work-related interactions with the teacher (for example, Galton *et al.*, 1980; Mortimore *et al.*, 1988) and that work-related talk with peers and other adults in the classroom increases motivation and concentration (Alexander, 1992).

Providing pupils with the optimum learning environment for the task in hand by ensuring that their seating arrangements reflect the need to work individually, cooperatively with others or as a whole class has also been the subject of recent debate. For example, research by Hastings (1995) suggests that pupils with poor attention spans may work better on individual tasks if seated in rows, L or U shapes. He emphasizes that seating these pupils appropriately in the first instance is preferable to moving them around when they become distracted by, or a distraction to, other pupils. He suggests that teachers might familiarize children with two or three classroom layouts for different activities claiming that teachers, who have tried this, find that the time spent moving furniture is more than compensated for by the improved quality of pupil work.

Within mixed ability classes, opportunities for productive talk and to draw on children's individual interests and aptitudes can be created by using cooperative groupwork. The jigsaw approach to cooperative groupwork, whereby each child makes his or her own specific contribution without which the task could not be completed, is particularly valuable in this respect. Studies on the effect on children of participating in different group compositions are rare. However, Bennett and Cass (1988) set up a study to contast the effects of three types of group; ability groups, mixed ability groups and groups containing only high and low attainers. All groups worked on the same task. They found high attainers performed well in all groups thereby challenging teachers' fears that grouping such children with low attainers adversely affects the more able. One low attainer working with two high attainers tended to be ignored but one high attainer working with two low attainers was much more successful. Fears that children with low ability working together might experience difficulty were well-founded and demonstrate the need for such groups to be given additional teacher help or support from a classroom assistant.

Most teachers make some use of ability grouping within their own classes especially in relation to mathematics, reading and other aspects of English. In response to the demands of the National Curriculum, in schools which are large enough to have parallel classes within a yeargroup, there appears to be an increasing willingness to try setting across classes for one or more of the core subjects. For this to be beneficial to all pupils it is generally necessary to deploy an extra teacher. This is to ensure that, if the group for those with learning difficulties and the group of highest attainers are kept small, this is not at the expense of those in the middle who, without an extra teacher, might have to be taught in an extremely large class. In the ATL sample schools we found no teachers who supported streaming. Streaming was viewed as an unjust system which both took minimal account of the fact that children often performed at different levels in different subjects and damaged their self-image at a very early age by labelling them as failures — a view supported by research into streaming (see, for example, Jackson, 1964).

One way in which pupils' motivation and confidence in themselves as learners can be promoted is through teaching children to become capable of managing, analysing and evaluating their own learning. In developing provision for pupils with SEN it will be useful to obtain their views and preferences regarding organizational features — such as within lesson support, withdrawal groups and ability grouping — teaching approaches and resources. Pupil involvement in the purpose and structuring of their work and in the evaluation of both the learning process and the outcomes are further encouraged within the revised National Curriculum, especially in English and design and technology — for example, at KS2 evaluating their design ideas and suggesting improvements. Greater participation by pupils in their education is also encouraged by the Code which advocates that 'schools make every effort to identify the ascertainable views and wishes of the child or young person about his or her current and future education' (p.14). It envisages pupils as expressing their opinions and wishes at all five stages of the assessment process, in the annual review of statements and at 14-plus when a transition plan is to be drawn up for their move into adult life.

In the ATL research sample we saw examples of teachers sharing the purpose behind tasks with children and helping them to understand and to contribute to the criteria by which their work would be assessed. This was achieved through, when being shown completed work, asking questions such as 'Well what do you think of it?' 'What do you like about it?' and 'How could you make it better?'. Also, by giving children evaluation sheets to fill in when tasks were completed. For younger children or those with reading difficulties the questions and alternative responses were represented pictorially. Alternatively teachers asked children to write about 'what went well and what did not'. For example, one teacher helped pupils to photograph their technology models and then to write an evaluation of the process of making the models and the finished product. These were then put into a class book which served as a record of their technology project.

We saw some examples of pupils taking responsibility not only for their own learning but also for the learning of others. For example, where children were working in pairs to write poems on dragons, they were correcting each other's spelling and sentence construction. In a Y4/5/6 class in a primary school, some children were writing individual stories about a mystery object. When they had finished their first drafts, they worked in pairs and, taking it in turns, each acted as a 'critical friend' and gave advice as to how both the content and style of the story could be improved. In small schools younger and older pupils were sometimes asked to work together in ways which promoted their intellectual development and improved their self-image. Older children of all abilities were asked to provide explanations, assistance and resources for younger ones. The younger ones used the older ones and their work as sources of information and models for what they would be able to achieve.

Another way in which teachers provided additional learning opportunities and increased differentiation (the focus of the next section), especially for pupils with SEN, was through additional classroom support, such as the use of part-time staff, teachers' aides and volunteer helpers. Depending on the qualifications and skills of the helper, supporting adults were used:

- to work with individuals, such as listening to reading and talking through work set;
- to work with pairs of children, such as supporting them in the use of IT or supervising practical activities;
- to work with a group to provide extra help in carrying out the instructions of a whole-class task;
- to circulate around the class helping those experiencing difficulties; and
- to observe for assessment purposes or to free the class teacher to do so.

Classroom assistants can be an invaluable source of help in modifying materials to improve differentiation and in providing children with another adult on whom to test out their ideas and who can clarify tasks. However, as documented by Tricker (1992), the planning and organizing of such contributions and managing personal relationships makes additional demands on class teachers and needs to be carefully thought through.

Since the publication of the Plowden Report (1967), which stressed the importance of home–school links in the primary school, the role of parents in assisting their children's learning has increasingly been recognized (see, for example, Mortimore *et al.*, 1988) and 'good practice' identified (see, for example, Jowett *et al.*, 1991). Through improved communications with parents and a wide range of initiatives — such as curriculum displays and workshops for parents, shared reading and writing schemes, pupil homework diaries and the involvement of parents in their children's records of achievement — parents are encouraged to be partners in helping their children to learn. Parental involvement receives prominance in the Code, although it gets only a brief mention in the final report of the Dearing Review (Dearing, 1993) which merely encourages schools to 'work closely with parents when defining individual curriculum content which addresses breadth, balance and special educational needs' (p.54). As increasingly children with a variety of special needs are integrated into primary schools, it is essential that teachers develop their skills of working in partnership with parents in order to be able to provide the support and practical advice that they need in the ways described by Hornby (1995).

### Differentiation

Lewis (1995) found that the largest category of INSET required in relation to pupils with SEN was in relation to differentiation. Differentiation is an area which requires whole school consideration in order to make explicit teachers' concerns and to bring together their relevant experience and ideas. By differentiation is meant:

> the identification of, and effective provision for, a range of abilities in one classroom, such that pupils in a particular class need not study the same things at the same pace and in the same way at all times. Differentiated approaches should mean that the needs of the very able, and of children with learning difficulties, are discerned and met. (Scottish Education Department, quoted in Simpson, 1989, p.73)

Since the introduction of the National Curriculum, differentiation — often undefined and open to a range of interpretations — has been advocated increasingly in policy documents at national, local and school level. The school-based assessment and IEPs contained within the Code further emphasize the need to differentiate curriculum provision in order that children with SEN can fully participate in individual, group and whole class activities.

While differentiation is particularly important for promoting the learning and boosting the confidence of pupils with SEN it is not solely or even mainly an SEN issue. As the overwhelming majority of primary school classes are mixed ability, teachers have always recognized the importance of providing a diversity of learning activities to meet the different learning needs of pupils. However, getting the correct match between the intellectual, manual and affective demand of tasks and pupils' abilities has proved difficult in practice for even those teachers recognized as being particularly effective (see, for example, Bennett *et al.*, 1984; Simpson, 1989).

The introduction of the National Curriculum and its associated assessment were viewed initially as likely to improve differentiation by increasing teachers' awareness of the level of attainment of individuals in each subject and providing a 10-level framework within which to plan for progression. However, in a 1990 conference address Richards, when reflecting on data collected on the early implementation of the National Curriculum through HMI inspections, reports:

> Differentiation of work continues to be a thorny and, in one sense, an insoluble problem. It is a pipedream, it is an impossible goal to differentiate work to suit the individual pupils' needs across the range of the curriculum. Nevertheless, steps can be taken to improve, to some degree or another, differentiation of work, even if within the limits of the possible rather than the desirable. (Reported by Campbell, 1990, p.11)

It is therefore, perhaps, unsurprising that OFSTED (1995) found work set across the primary and secondary sector to be inadequately matched to the ability of the children, often rendering lessons inaccessible to pupils with learning difficulties. In primary schools:

> pupils with special educational needs but without statements were poorly served by such provision in two-thirds of the lessons they attended. Poor match of tasks to their abilities often had an adverse effect on the attitudes shown by pupils in lessons. (OFSTED, 1995, p.28)

Differentiation can increase pupil understanding, motivation, enjoyment and confidence in learning. Therefore, as Richards suggests, it is important to look for manageable ways forward to effect improvements.

Data from the ATL research revealed how differentiation was being tackled in the sample schools. The approaches used most frequently were:

- the provision for the able of additional more demanding work in the same area once they had completed that set for the class;
- the allocation of completely different activities for groups and individual pupils of different abilities; and
- setting the same task for all pupils but expecting a range of outcomes in terms of speed of task completion, quality and quantity of work and the amount of help required.

Other fairly common approaches to differentiation that were observed were:

- the use of individualized schemes, especially in mathematics and English grammar, and the use of computer programmes; and
- menu arrangements whereby pupils selected tasks from a range of possibilities and completed them in the order that they preferred and at their own pace.

In both of these approaches differentiation is achieved through individualization of the curriculum. While in some lessons this may be the most appropriate approach, it involves time-consuming preparation and classroom management is very demanding if all the class are working on individual tasks. Also, the frequent setting of individual work could serve to isolate pupils with SEN from their peers and deny them the opportunity of sharing experiences and learning cooperatively. Webster *et al.* (1994) suggest that 'pre-tutoring' (assisting children in advance of the task to develop or consolidate the skills and concepts to be required) and 'post-tutoring' (offering individual feedback on strengths and weaknesses and explanations of any areas of misunderstanding) can greatly assist children with SEN to work on the same tasks as their peers.

A task may be differentiated through the way in which it is accessed by pupils, the process involved in task completion or in terms of the outcome or finished product. Each form of differentiation can be used singularly or in combination.

1   An example of differentiation by access was when a science task was presented to a class in the form of a worksheet but a support teacher explained the task to two boys with learning difficulties. Other ways of enabling pupils with reading difficulties to access the same task as their peers might be to provide instructions on audio tape and/or in pictorial or diagramatic form.

2   An example of a task which was modified to differentiate the processes involved was in a technology lesson where all the children were asked to make the same model but were given different materials with which to construct it. Task processes can also be modified through supplying different degrees of teacher assistance — for example in story-writing additional assistance could be provided through: the provision of vocabulary and spellings; additional stimuli for ideas; putting the child's ideas into written sentences and the ongoing reading through together and correction of drafts.

3   The end product or response can be differentiated through the use of alternative forms of presentation of what has been learned. Hence information gleaned from a television programme might be reported orally, through a cartoon strip, the completion of a worksheet or in a written account.

The use of graded tasks for individuals or groups, other than those available through commercial schemes, was viewed as a more complex approach which demanded generally too much preparation time for it to occur regularly. First, an analysis of the task into small steps was required. Second, pupils' current mastery of these steps had to be diagnosed. Third, activities had to be planned focusing on one or combinations of these steps tailored to the diagnosed needs of individuals or groups. A simple example of graded tasks was the use of a set of handwriting activities and cards in a Year 3 class. Such an approach can have particular value for pupils with learning difficulties because if tasks are composed of smaller identifiable steps then pupils can experience more immediate success and recognize that they are making progress.

In addition to 'proactive differentiation' which is planned, two teacher researchers who carried out observations of history and geography lessons identified 'reactive differentiation' (National Primary Centre, 1995). Reactive differentiation occurs 'when teachers make a direct intervention with a child or group as a result of a perceived difficulty with a piece of learning or as a response to difficult behaviour' (p.26). While such interventions can be very demanding of teacher time, energy and initiative, the researchers concluded that 'many teachers are very competent at this type of differentiation, even though they rarely recognized it as such' (p.26). However, they found 'some teachers who either did not recognize learning difficulties experienced by children or who were unable to offer intervention that would enhance their learning' (p.26).

Differentiation could usefully be the focus of a school-based meeting, workshop or INSET session called to identify and/or to consolidate and build on what has been achieved. A starting point might be to ask colleagues to review their teaching for one afternoon and to identify the ways in which they had differentiated the tasks set and to explore additional possibilities that they might have tried. Alternatively, differentiation for two particular children with very different SEN might be brainstormed by staff in the light of one teacher's weekly plans for a particular subject or aspect of topic work. A useful resource to inform discussion during such a session is the National Primary Centre's (1995) publication on differentiation resulting from a school-based project in three LEAs. It poses questions for reviewing practice and gives examples of alternative approaches to differentiation through short case studies. Further detailed examples of differentiation in both primary and secondary schools, which could also stimulate discussion, are provided in a handbook on differentiation compiled by the National Council for Educational Technology (Dickinson and Wright, 1993).

## Conclusion

While supporting the principle of entitlement for all pupils to the whole curriculum including the National Curriculum, working to achieve this is proving extremely demanding in a context of increasing pressures, rising class size, diminishing resources — especially teacher time — and inadequate specialist training in the recognition of the wide range of special educational needs pupils may experience. However, primary teachers are committed to promoting the academic progress and social and affective development of each individual in their classes. To achieve this means employing a range of teaching techniques and types of tasks and experimenting with alternative forms of curriculum and classroom organization. However, a classroom environment which enables pupils with SEN to make progress and to enjoy and derive satisfaction from their learning will be a classroom which maximizes the learning and achievements of all pupils.

There is considerable concern as to whether the Code of Practice can be effectively implemented. The Government's failure to finance its implementation, contractions in the resources of many support services, minimal provision of training both for SENCOs and classteachers, lack of non-contact time for SENCOs and uncertainty as to the competence of governors with a SEN remit all combine to limit its chances of success. However, it has been generally welcomed and viewed as a potentially powerful mechanism for a more coherent, thorough and speedier approach to catering for children's special educational needs. Undoubtedly, it has moved SEN issues and provision to the top of the agenda of priorities in many primary schools and ensured its incorporation in the School Development Plan and formed the focus of staff and governor meetings and in-service training held to support that plan.

SENCOs are central to the successful formulation and implementation of a school's SEN policy and in the improved classroom provision for pupils with SEN. If best practice is to be recognized and implemented by all staff, SENCOs need to provide moral support, practical advice and up-to-date information for their colleagues, and to encourage them to share concerns and to disseminate their ideas and successes. As one SENCO put it: 'It's a role which can be difficult, exhausting and sometimes frustrating, but also very satisfying'.

## References

ALEXANDER, R. (1992) *Policy and Practice in Primary Education*, London, Routledge.
ALEXANDER, R., ROSE, J. and WOODHEAD, C. (1992) *Curriculum Organisation and Classroom Practice: A Discussion Paper*, London, DES.
AUDIT COMMISSION (1992a) *Getting in on the Act*, London, HMSO.
AUDIT COMMISSION (1992b) *Getting the Act Together*, London, HMSO.
BENNETT, N. and CASS, A. (1988) 'The effects of group composition on group interactive processes and pupil understanding', *British Educational Research Journal*, **15**, pp.19–32.
BENNETT, N., DESFORGES, C., COCKBURN, A. and WILKINSON, B. (1984) *The Quality of Pupil Learning Experiences*, London, Lawrence Erlbaum Associates.
BUCHANAN, M. (1995) 'What are the implications of the 1993 Education Act for special educational needs coordinators in ordinary primary schools?', Unpublished MA assignment, University of York.
CAMPBELL, R.J. (1990) 'Children and subjects: A national perspective', Summary of paper presented by Colin Richards, in 'Papers from the third annual conference of the association for the study of primary education', Wolverhampton Polytechnic, 14–15 September.
CAMPBELL, R.J. (1994) 'Manageability and control of the primary curriculum', in SOUTHWORTH, G. (Ed) *Readings in Primary School Development*, London, Falmer Press.
DEARING, R. (1993) *The National Curriculum and its Assessment, Final Report*, London, SCAA.

Department for Education (1994) *Code of Practice on the Identification and Assessment of Special Educational Needs*, London, DfE.

Dickinson, C. and Wright, J. (1993) *Differentiation: A Practical Handbook of Classroom Strategies*, Coventry, National Council for Educational Technology.

Gains, C. (1994) 'Editorial', *Support for Learning*, **9**, 3, p.102.

Galton, M., Simon, B. and Croll, P. (1980) *Inside the Primary Classroom*, London, Routledge and Kegan Paul.

Garner, P. (1995) 'Sense or nonsense?: Dilemmas in the SEN code of practice', *Support for Learning*, **10**, 1, pp.3–7.

Harvey, J. (1995) 'The role of the special educational needs coordinator at Marton Grove Primary School', *Support for Learning*, **10**, 2, pp.79–82.

Hastings, N. (1995) 'Seats of learning?', *Support for Learning*, **10**, 1, pp.8–11.

Hornby, G. (1995) *Working with Parents of Children with Special Needs*, London, Cassell.

Jackson, B. (1964) *Streaming: An Education System in Miniature*, London, Routledge and Kegan Paul.

Jowett, S., Baginsky, M. and MacNeil, M. (1991) *Building Bridges: Parental Involvement in Schools*, Windsor, NFER-Nelson.

Lewis, A. (1995) *Special Needs Provision in Mainstream Primary Schools*, ASPE paper, **6**, Chester, ASPE/Trentham Books.

Mortimore, P., Sammons, P., Stoll, L., Lewis, D. and Ecob, R. (1988) *School Matters: The Junior Years*, Wells, Open Books.

Moss, G. (1994) 'The role of the SENCO', *Special Children*, **78**, pp.1–8.

National Curriculum Council (1989) *A Curriculum for All, Curriculum Guidance 2*, York, NCC.

National Primary Centre (1995) *Differentiation in Practice*, Oxford, NPC.

OFSTED (1995) *The Annual Report of Her Majesty's Chief Inspector of Schools: Part 1*, London, HMSO.

Peter, M. (1995) 'Wise men or blind mice', *Times Educational Supplement*, 14 April, p.35.

Pike, G. and Selby, D. (1988) *Global Teacher, Global Learner*, London, Hodder and Stoughton.

Simpson, M. (1989) *Differentiation in the Primary School: Classroom Perspectives*, Aberdeen and Dundee, Northern College.

Stevens, C. (1994) 'The National Curriculum review, SEN teachers talk back to SCAA', *Special*, Autumn, pp.29–30.

Stevens, C. (1995) 'In search of a sense of achievement', *Times Educational Supplement*, 14 April.

Tricker, M. (1992) 'Support work in primary classrooms: Some management concerns', in Vulliamy, G. and Webb, R. (Eds) *Teacher Research and Special Educational Needs*, London, David Fulton.

Visser, J. (Ed) (1994) *A Guide to the 1994 Code of Practice, OFSTED Inspections and Related Documents*, Stafford, NASEN Enterprises Ltd.

Webb, R. (1993) *Eating the Elephant Bit by Bit: The National Curriculum at Key Stage 2*, London, ATL.

Webb, R. (1994) *After the Deluge: Changing Roles and Responsibilities in the Primary School*, London, ATL.

Webb, R. and Vulliamy, G. (1996) *Roles and Responsibilities in the Primary School: Changing Demands, Changing Practices*, Buckingham, Open University Press.

Webster, A., Webster, V., Moon, C. and Warwick, A. (1994) *Supporting Learning in the Primary School, Meeting Individual Needs under the New Code of Practice*, Bristol, Avec Design and Consultancy Publishers.

*Chapter 2*

# Analysing Classroom Discipline

*Pamela Munn*

### Introduction

It is Monday morning and Mrs Smith meets her class of twenty-five 8-year-olds for the first time.

**Mrs Smith**    Good morning everybody. I've heard some very good things about you from Miss Reid and I'm looking forward to getting to know you. I know we are all going to get along well together. I'd like us to start by deciding what our classroom rules are going to be. . .
I'd like each group to decide on one really important rule and say why it is important. . .

There can hardly be a more important aspect of teaching than classroom discipline. Creating and sustaining a classroom environment which promotes learning is fundamental to the job. Yet classroom discipline is not just a means to an end, the end being that children learn. It is an end in itself. The way in which power and authority are exercised, rules established and infringements of rules dealt with are important elements in children's personal and social development. Children will probably remember the values displayed through a teacher's approach to classroom discipline, long after the content of a particular piece of academic work has been forgotten. Classroom discipline, then, is about much more than time on task and rules and sanctions. It is about roles and relationships, between teacher and pupil and among pupils themselves.

In the example above Mrs Smith is transmitting a number of messages to her pupils:

- she has high expectations of them ('I've heard very good things about you');
- she regards them as people ('I'm looking forward to getting to know you');
- she is interested in their views (the group exercise); and
- she values people working together (the group exercise).

Experienced teachers like Mrs Smith have a fund of skills, knowledge and expertise about classroom discipline, but they rarely make this explicit. It is part of the taken-for-grantedness of being a teacher and seldom discussed or analysed once initial training and the early years of teaching are over. This is a pity because thinking about what you do to promote effective discipline in the classroom can have a number of benefits:

- it can help experienced teachers become even more expert in their use of particular strategies as they make explicit what works for them and why it works;
- it can raise awareness about the values messages being transmitted, perhaps unconsciously, in the classroom;
- it can increase the opportunities of learning from others by sharing experiences of success and failure with colleagues thereby promoting teaching as a collaborative rather than a private activity; and
- it can be particularly helpful to new teachers who do not have the repertoire of skills and knowledge of their more experienced colleagues to draw on in promoting good discipline or in dealing with indiscipline.

This chapter aims to encourage teachers to analyse their practice and to work collaboratively in doing so.[1,2] The suggested framework for analysis derives from a study of experienced teachers about their practice (Munn, Johnstone and Chalmers, 1992). This study concentrated on a small number of schools and teachers. It involved observing real teachers in action and asking them about what they did to get their pupils to work well. The intention is to go beyond traditional texts offering useful advice and tips for teachers, to provide a way of thinking about classroom discipline which helps teachers understand their own classrooms, and the logic and rationale underlying their practice. This approach is based on the simple belief that it is a good thing for teachers to think about and to analyse their practice. It is through understanding what you do and why you do it that improvement is most likely. Before introducing this framework, let us glance briefly at previous research on classroom discipline.

## Previous Research

There is no shortage of excellent texts on classroom management and control. Many of these are aimed at new teachers and provide helpful checklists encouraging teachers to think about their practice and to analyse situations where discipline works well or where discipline is a problem. (For reviews see Docking, 1987; Graham, 1988; Johnstone and Munn, 1987 and Topping, 1983). There is, of course, no infallible recipe for achieving good discipline in the classroom. If one existed, we would surely have found it by now. We do know from research, however, that there are a number of features which are likely to promote good discipline. These are:

- advance preparation and planning which takes into account children's aptitudes and interests;
- positive teacher–pupil relationships, where children's self esteem is valued; and
- a belief that teachers and schools can make a difference to children's behaviour.

These are ideals to which almost all teachers would subscribe but they can be hard to put into practice in the hurly burly of classroom life. Nevertheless, an awareness of the circumstances which encourage these ideals and of the circumstances making them difficult is important for teachers. As we will see below, one of the benefits of the framework for analysing practice is to heighten awareness of these circumstances.

Research has also shown that there are specific things which teachers can do to achieve good discipline. These include:

- a prompt start to lessons;
- clear instructions to pupils;
- consistency about standards;
- knowledge of materials to be used and having them ready in advance;
- using praise and rewards; and
- being mobile; walking around the class as a way of being alert to what pupils are doing.

The complex and uncertain business of teaching means that a quest for a menu of effective strategies and sanctions for maintaining effective discipline is naive, if such a menu is regarded as an infallible guide to success. This is not to suggest that every teacher needs to reinvent the wheel. It is to suggest that strategies and sanctions are possibilities, to be experimented with. It is worth noting that very similar messages arise from research on primary and secondary classrooms. A key feature of good discipline is the emphasis on positive pupil–teacher relationships (Bird *et al.*, 1981; Tattum, 1982; Wragg, 1993; Emmer *et al.*, 1984; Kyriacou, 1986). This view tends to be echoed by pupils themselves, even disaffected pupils (Nash, 1976; Docking, 1980; Watkins and Wagner, 1987). Pupils' ideal teachers tend to be firm and fair, help them to learn through clear explanations and treat pupils as people.

Although this chapter concentrates on classroom discipline, it is important to remember that the school as a whole sends messages to pupils about how they are valued. There is an extensive literature on this. Although much of this literature relates to features of secondary schooling, there are important implications in it for primary schools. Implications concerning curriculum organization and provision, for instance, are relevant in thinking about how pupils are allocated to classes and to groups within classes. The literature highlights the following factors associated with teacher–pupil relations: 'curriculum provision', in particular the availability of the same curriculum for all pupils (Hargreaves, 1982; Lawrence *et al.*, 1984; Sharp, 1981); 'curriculum organization', the setting or streaming associated with anti-school subcultures (Hargreaves, 1967; 1976; Lacey, 1970; Willis, 1977; Ball, 1981) and the manner in which teachers apply, and pupils respond to, 'systems of rules, sanctions and rewards' (Munn *et al.*, 1992; Docking, 1987). Often related to these features are teachers' expectations about their pupils, their perceptions of their pupils' ability and socio-economic status (Reynolds, 1992) and the extent to which teachers and pupils share a value system about school purposes and processes (Munn *et al.*, 1992; Johnstone and Munn, 1992; Hill, 1991; Reynolds *et al.*, 1987). It is worth highlighting these larger factors which affect classroom discipline because it draws attention to the ways in which many of the taken-for-granted features of school life can impact positively or negatively on children and contribute to a general disciplinary climate in the school. It is within this general climate that classroom discipline operates.

## Analysing Discipline in Your Classroom

Classrooms are busy places and it is not easy to stand back from day to day activities and to analyse why something went well or went badly. Teachers think about their work a good deal, of course, and often share good and bad experiences with colleagues over a cup of coffee in the staff room at breaks. Such shared experience can be a way of letting off steam or of raising spirits when troublesome pupils respond positively to something and show a new side to themselves. What follows is one way of putting that shared experience into a framework to let patterns in that experience show through. By uncovering such patterns teachers can come to understand more about their own classroom practice and, if they have good working relationships with colleagues, can share their practice with others. To my way of thinking, it is through such an exchange of experience and, crucially through exploring ideas about why things turned out the way they did, that improvement in practice is promoted. As mentioned in the introduction, it is also important that student teachers get access to the tacit knowledge of experienced teachers about how they manage discipline in their classrooms.

The framework for analysing classroom practice has three main parts to it, your 'actions' as the class teacher, the 'classroom context' in which you find yourself; and the 'goals' you have for the class, or groups or individual pupils. Each of these parts affects the other but let us start by looking at each in turn. The starting point for examining each of these parts is a group of pupils whom you particularly enjoy teaching and with whom you experience few if any discipline problems. Focus on your most recent contact with this group. The aim is to understand why this group works well. Then, go on to contrast this experience with your experience of a group you find troublesome.

*Actions*

It can be helpful to divide actions into two broad categories, those which you take in advance of meeting the group of pupils you are analysing and those which are reactions to events as they unfold. Advance planning and preparation are very important in minimizing opportunities for disruption to occur. Examples of advance planning which the teachers in our study talked about were;

- ensuring equipment and materials needed were to hand and in working order;
- being in command of the subject matter;
- making links with what had gone before;
- thinking through what would interest and motivate the pupils (this meant knowing them pretty well);
- being clear what classroom rules were, in terms of, for instance, talking, getting up out of seats, collecting equipment, tidying away, exiting from the classroom etc., and
- negotiating rules with pupils and pupils being clear why rules were needed.

In other words, teachers talked a great deal about how to create an atmosphere in which the expectation was that pupils would behave well and engage in purposeful learning. Teachers went about this in different ways, reflecting their own beliefs and values and taking school policy into account. The key point, however, is that they planned ahead and stressed that prevention was better than cure.

One feature that many teachers had in common was the negotiation of classroom rules. The teachers in our study said that it was important to have only a few rules, having many rules just created opportunities for pupils to break them. Moreover, rules expressed positively, as in 'be polite' created an expectation of good behaviour rather than a list of negatives which set up the kinds of things that pupils had to be stopped from doing. Explaining the reason for rules was seen as important too. We found that pupils generally accepted rules which they saw as reasonable. For instance typical comments were, 'If we talk and carry on we will not know the work we should know.' 'People would get hurt if you ran in corridors.' Pupils were resentful of rules for which there was no explanation beyond the teacher saying that they had to be obeyed.

As well as advance planning and preparation, teachers react to events. There is, of course, an extensive repertoire of reactions to signs that all is not well. None of these will come as a surprise to teachers. They include:

- verbal rebukes;
- warnings;
- standing beside a pupil;
- moving a pupil;
- using humour to defuse a situation;
- explaining and helping a pupil who is 'stuck';
- sending pupils to a higher authority; and
- involving parents.

The kind of reaction largely depends on the nature of the offence. There are, however, some well known maxims about reactions to indiscipline which are drawn from the importance of positive pupil–teacher relationships in promoting good discipline. These include the following;

- criticize the behaviour not the pupil;
- avoid blaming the whole class;
- private rebukes are usually more effective than public ones where loss of face of one of the parties involved can mean that future relationships have to deal with the experience of public humiliation;
- avoid comparison with other pupils or reference to other family members;
- be seen to be fair and consistent; and
- do not make threats which you are not prepared to carry out.

Rather than present an exhaustive list of reactions to indiscipline, however, the aim of this section is to help you analyse the different kinds of actions you use with the group of pupils whom you enjoy teaching. Then you are asked to repeat the exercise focusing on a group of pupils you find troublesome.

*Table 2.1: Practical activity 1*

---

- Think back to your most recent work with a group of pupils you enjoy teaching. Jot down what you did to get them to work well. Looking at what you have written, how many actions would you categorize as advance planning and preparation? How many would you see as reacting to potential or actual disruption? What is the balance between advance planning and preparation and reacting? Is the balance one that you are happy with? If not, what can you do to change matters? Now do the same thing for the troublesome group. What are the main similarities and differences?

- This first stage of analysis describes *what* you did. The next stage is to analyse *why* you took these actions. Unless you understand why you took certain actions you will not have much chance of changing the pattern or of unravelling why you are more successful with some groups than others. This brings us to the classroom context.

---

### The Classroom Context

The context in which teachers work greatly affects what they do to promote and sustain effective discipline. Classrooms are part of schools and schools exist in local communities. These have their own histories which undoubtedly influence what counts as effective discipline. In concentrating on the classroom context, therefore, it is important to remember the 'bigger picture' of schools, parents and children and local communities in which the classroom is situated. It is also important to remember that teachers are people too and their own histories, attitudes, beliefs and moods will influence what they see as indiscipline and what they do to deal with it.

Teachers have identified many features of the classroom context which affect discipline. These range from the physical layout of the room, the state of repair of the furniture and the time of day, to the topics being taught and the size of the class. Some features, or classroom conditions, cannot be changed. Friday afternoon will always be Friday afternoon. Others may be changed, such as the composition of groups or the sequencing of particular curriculum content. The important thing is to be aware of the features which influence discipline in your classroom. Once you understand what these are, you can take account of them both in advance preparation and planning and in the ways in which you react to disruption. For example, if Friday afternoons are typically difficult because of the prospect of freedom from school over the weekend, you could plan special treats or activities which would encourage children to look forward to Fridays as a special time. The particular treats will vary from teacher to teacher. The important point is that there is recognition of a particular condition which affects discipline and that this influence is taken into account in curriculum planning.

The most important condition influencing every teacher's classroom discipline is the pupils themselves. This is hardly surprising. What is more difficult is to unpack the beliefs and expectations a teacher has about his/her pupils and to be aware that these beliefs and expectations are conveyed in all kinds of subtle ways to the pupils themselves. This in turn can influence the pupils' behaviour in the classroom. The following extract from a group interview with some 4–5-year-olds illustrates that the so called hidden curriculum is very obvious to some of them. The interviewer has been asking about what the children do in class.

| **Lorna** (to Gordon) | We're in the Yellow group! |
| **Gordon** | Which is top. |
| **Billy and interviewer** | |
| (together) | How do you know? |
| **Gordon** | Because we always do all the real assignments first and then we do all the rubbish. |
| **Lorna** | He means all the gluing and stuff. |
| **Interviewer** | Thinking about your class, what is a real assignment? |
| **Gordon** | Well, reading. |
| **Others** | Maths/sound book/jotter/reading. |

Gordon, aged 5, knows he is in the top group and associates this with valuing academic work above craft work such as gluing. Now it is impossible to tell if this value came from home or school but it is clear that other children as well as Gordon are able to distinguish 'real' work from other work. The point is the evidence that children pick up very quickly all kinds of messages from teachers and others about what is valued and what is expected of them.

Teachers clearly have a good deal of knowledge about their pupils, their aptitudes and abilities, their interests and enthusiasms, and often about their home circumstances. They also have knowledge about how their class works as a class and about how groups of pupils work together. This kind of knowledge is a powerful and indeed important and necessary influence on teaching. It is often used tacitly and made explicit only by someone asking why a particular action was taken as in the example below. The teacher explains her finely balanced interest in a pupil's holiday in terms of letting the pupil know she had missed her in class and her knowledge that the rest of the class could be jealous at the amount of attention being given to a particular pupil.

> I had to speak to Susan, let her know I noticed she was back from holiday — but I didn't want to make too much of it. After all, the others in the class could be jealous. Not all of them have parents who could afford a holiday.

There are many influences on teachers' actions as the practical activity in Table 2.2 will show. Understanding what they are and how they affect what you do is the next step towards promoting good discipline.

The brief example in Table 2.3 shows how a teacher's knowledge about his or her pupils and mood can influence actions. No value judgment is intended with this brief example. It merely serves to illustrate an approach to analysing the influences on actions with the aim of raising consciousness about what you do and why. It can be difficult for teachers to make explicit the expectations they have about their pupils and how these influence actions. Being honest with yourself is clearly important. The description and analysis of actions is best done with a helpful and supportive colleague. If you had a trusted colleague, he or she could help by discussing your analysis of practice or by observing you in action in the classroom and discussing afterwards your actions, the influences on them and the consequences of the actions for discipline and the values messages which were being transmitted.

### Goals

So far the emphasis has been on actions, preparation and planning and reactions to disruption. The likely influences on actions have also been mentioned. The suggestion is that if you can recognize these influences, face them and consider their effect on what you do, then you will begin to understand what

*Table 2.2: Practical activity 2*

Think about the group of pupils you described earlier, the group you enjoy teaching. What are, for you, the most important influences on your actions for this group? Think in terms of both your advance planning and preparation and how you react when disruption or threat of disruption occurs. The following list is a short example to get you started.

### Influences on advance planning: Some examples

- you feel confident about the topic — so you know what the main teaching points will be;
- there is a good range of materials available — so you have these laid out in the classroom;
- you know that it will interest this group — so you begin by highlighting their interest;
- you have done this bit of work before — so you know roughly how much time it will take;
- other influences. . .

### Influences on reactions: Some examples

- your knowledge of the group — it usually works well together — you show disappointment rather than anger when it misbehaves;
- your mood — you feel happy and decide to crack a joke to defuse the situation;
- the time of year — you are forgiving of misbehaviour because it is near Christmas and there are many distractions

**or**

- your knowledge of the class as a whole — you shout at the whole class because if the pupils in the good group play up then the whole class will disintegrate;
- other influences. . .

---

*Table 2.3: Practical activity 3*

Once you have written down the main influences on your actions with the group of pupils you enjoy teaching, repeat the exercise for a troublesome group. An example is given below of how you might start.

| My actions | Key influences on actions | Good group | Troublesome group |
|---|---|---|---|
| • Had materials prepared and laid ready for use | Knew good material was available | Yes | Yes |
| • Had a quiet word with a pupil as he wasn't settling down to work | Paul is a hard worker. He probably didn't understand what he had to do | Yes | No |
| • Shouted at the whole group | That group never settle down — I'm fed up with them | No | Yes |

promotes good discipline in your particular classroom. However, there is one more feature of discipline that needs to be taken into account. This is the goals or purposes of your teaching. Your actions will be affected not only by the classroom context but also by what you hope to achieve with your pupils.

Teachers will have a number of different goals for their pupils. Some goals will concern their academic progress; others will concern their personal and social development. Goals will probably be expressed in very particular ways. For instance, a goal might be to finish a particular piece of work by lunchtime; or to get a shy pupil to contribute to a group discussion; or to make something in time for a special event and so on. Some goals will be explicit and contained in lesson plans but many will be implicit. Goals influence the way teachers act in classrooms. Analysing your goals and comparing them with the actions you took can be a salutary experience. Goals of valuing children and promoting their self-esteem can look very hollow when actions taken over a particular segment of teaching are analysed. For instance a teacher at the end of his or her tether may say to a troublesome pupil, 'I'm fed up with you. You're just like your brother. You can't do anything unless I tell you twenty times.' More subtly perhaps, the teacher's choice of only a few pupils to take responsibility for certain tasks can send messages about who is valued in the class. Thus the purpose of making your goals explicit and asking whether your actions were consistent with your goals can be helpful in analysing the good and bad times in terms of discipline in your classroom.

*Table 2.4: Practical activity 4*

Look back to the list of actions you took with the group you enjoy teaching. Jot down the answers to the following questions.

- What were the main goals for that group? How can they be described? For example, can they be divided into academic, personal and social development and other kinds of goals?
- Can particular actions be identified as appropriate and consistent with these goals?
- Do actions and goals conflict and if so how can this be explained?
- Are the goals appropriate for the pupils? If not, what should be changed — goals, actions or the classroom context? If the latter which aspects of the context can be changed?

Now repeat this exercise for a troublesome group of pupils or for an occasion when discipline became a problem. Do you see patterns emerging? Where are the main similarities and differences between the enjoyable group and the troublesome group in terms of goals — and goals and actions? An analysis of this kind should help you identify the things you do well and to learn from this and apply your knowledge to situations where things turn out less effectively than you would wish.

## Conclusion

This chapter has suggested that in order to maintain and improve classroom discipline teachers need to understand the mix of ingredients that contribute to it. This means going beyond the tips for teachers' approach to an analysis of *why* particular actions are effective and others less so. The aim has been to provide a framework which will help develop this understanding and make sense of the many and varied elements that go to make up effective discipline. Three key features have been highlighted:

- teachers' actions — distinguishing between advance planning and preparation and reacting to classroom events;
- the classroom context — weighing up the importance of the time of day, the physical layout of the room but most crucially the teacher's knowledge and expectations of pupils; and
- teachers' goals — suggesting that these need to be appropriate.

These features have been presented as separate and distinct in order to help teachers to analyse their practice. Of course, they interact. For instance, the kinds of goals which a teacher has for her pupils will largely be based on what she considers appropriate for their age and stage — goals about reading attainments for groups of 5-year-olds will be different from those for 11-year-olds. The actions she takes to promote these goals will depend on a large number of things, including beliefs about children's reading readiness, knowledge about the ways in which reading is encouraged, the time of day and year, what she knows about the particular pupils and so on. Actions themselves can change the classroom context — moving the furniture, rearranging pupil groups. They can also change goals — during project work, for instance, actions intended to promote independent learning such as having a range of resources available and letting pupils work at their own pace, might be transformed into actions that are more to do with whole class teaching if the teacher thinks that independent learning is not going well. In this situation there is an interplay of goals, the classroom context (signs that pupils are not making progress) and actions. The seeming simplicity of the framework disguises the complexity and fluidity of teachers' classroom decision making. Nevertheless it is offered as a starting point for analysing teachers' practice (see Figure 2.1).

The practical tasks suggest contrasting enjoyable and difficult groups or classroom occasions. Analysing one's own practice is never easy and yet this needs to be done to get beyond the 'try one thing and then another' approach. Many initial teacher education courses and many advanced courses for more experienced teachers aim to encourage teachers to reflect on their practice. Such courses offer one kind of supportive environment in which to carry out the practical exercises suggested. They could also be part of a school-based in-service programme organized by teachers themselves; if this is not possible groups of teachers interested in this area could get together to plan a series of discussions on actions, the classroom context and goals. A forum in which teachers can share their analyses and develop ideas can be very helpful.

It is also worth stressing that the emphasis on school-based initial teacher education can be a stimulus to experienced teachers to reflect upon their

Figure 2.1:  Teachers' practice: Actions

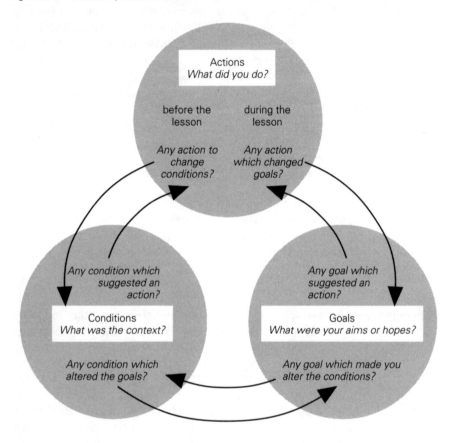

practice as a way of helping new teachers to learn. This reflection in turn can encourage the professional development of experienced teachers themselves if they take a critical and analytic perspective on what they do.

Finally, it is worth re-emphasizing that effective classroom discipline is a means to an end — purposeful and enjoyable learning, but it is also an end in itself — part of the personal and social development of children and young people. Through the way in which teachers establish and maintain discipline, children and young people come to learn something about power and authority, about roles and relationships and about values. One of the most memorable comments made by a pupil in our research on discipline was the following:

I really like [my teacher]. He makes me feel like a person.

As Pring (1985) has argued, one of the central tasks of teachers is to help students become human. He puts forward a case to show that 'conceptual sense can be made of personal and social education as a curriculum aim and that broad aims can be translated into practical terms, just as in any other area of the curriculum' (p.167). He also argues, however, that personal, moral and social development must not be so narrowly focused on the overt curriculum that we neglect the wider social values that are transmitted through schooling. Teachers' classroom discipline, then, is a powerful transmitter of these social values. Teachers who reflect on this aspect of their work, are, therefore, not only engaged in a task that will add to their technical competence but in a task that goes right to the heart of what teaching is about. This is one reason for the central importance of classroom discipline in the professional development of teachers.

## Notes

1 This chapter derives from a research grant from the Scottish Office Education Department (SOED) on discipline in Scottish primary and secondary schools carried out under the auspices of the Scottish Council for Research in Education (SCRE). The research was undertaken with Margaret Johnstone and Valerie Chalmers. I am grateful to all for their help. Responsibility for the content lies with me. The views represented here are not necessarily those of SOED or of SCRE. The research reports arising from the project are listed in the references. The SOED also funded the development of separate support packs on discipline for primary and secondary schools and some of the ideas contained in these packs are extended and developed here. I am grateful to SOED for permission to do so and also for granting permission to reproduce the diagram of Figure 2.1.

2 The following resources are suggested as starting points for those wishing to take further the ideas in this chapter:

McLean, A. (1992) *Promoting Positive Behaviour in the Primary School*, Glasgow, Faculty of Education, Strathclyde University, Jordanhill Campus.

Munn, P., Johnstone, M., Watson, G. and Edwards, L. (1993) *Action on Discipline: A Support Pack for Primary Schools*, Edinburgh, SCRE (This pack contains information about resource materials on discipline as well practical activities for classroom and school discipline.)

Pollard, A. and Tann, S. (1993) (2nd ed.) *Reflective Teaching in the Primary School*, London, Cassell.

## References

Ball, S.J. (1981) *Beachside Comprehensive*, Cambridge, Cambridge University Press.

Bird, C., Chessum, R., Furlong, J. and Johnston, D. (1981) 'Disaffected pupils', Educational Studies Unit, Department of Government, Brunel University.

Docking, J.W. (1980) *Control and Discipline in Schools*, London, Harper and Row.

Docking, J.W. (1987) *Control and Discipline in Schools: Perspectives and Approaches*, London, Harper and Row.

Emmer, E.T., Evertson, C.M., Sandford, J.P., Clements, B.S. and Worsham, M. (1984) *Classroom Management for Secondary Teachers*, New Jersey, Prentice Hall.

Graham, J. (1988) *Schools, Disruptive Behaviour and Delinquency*, London, Home Office Research Study 96, HMSO.

*Pamela Munn*

HARGREAVES, D.H. (1967) *Social Relations in a Secondary School*, London, Routledge and Kegan Paul.

HARGREAVES, D.H. (1976) 'Reactions to labelling', in HAMERSLEY, M. and WOODS, P. (Eds) *The Process of Schooling: A Sociological Reader*, London, Routledge and Kegan Paul/Open University Press.

HARGREAVES, D.H. (1982) *The Challenge for the Comprehensive School*, London, Routledge and Kegan Paul.

HILL, B.V. (1991) *Values Education in Australian Schools*, Victoria, ACER.

JOHNSTONE, M. and MUNN, P. (1987) *Discipline in Schools: A Review of 'Causes' and 'Cures'*, Edinburgh, SCRE.

JOHNSTONE, M. and MUNN, P. (1992) *Discipline in Scottish Secondary Schools*, Edinburgh, SCRE.

KYRIACOU, C. (1986) *Effective Teaching in Schools*, Oxford, Basil Blackwell.

LACEY, C. (1970) *Hightown Grammar: The School as a Social System*, Manchester, Manchester University Press.

LAWRENCE, J., STEEL, D. and YOUNG, P. (1984) *Disruptive Children: Disruptive Schools?*, London, Croom Helm.

MUNN, P., JOHNSTONE, M. and CHALMERS, V. (1992) *Effective Discipline in Primary Schools and Classrooms*, London, Paul Chapman.

NASH, R. (1976) 'Pupil expectations of their teachers', in STUBBS, M. and DELAMONT, S. (Eds) *Explorations in Classroom Observations*, London, Wiley.

PRING, R. (1985) *Personal and Social Education in the Curriculum*, London, Hodder-Stoughton.

REYNOLDS, D. (1992) 'School effectiveness and school improvement: An updated review of the British literature', in REYNOLDS, D. and CUTTANCE, P. (Eds) (1992) *School Effectiveness: Research, Policy and Practice*, London, Cassell.

REYNOLDS, D., SULLIVAN, M. and MURGATROYD, S.J. (1987) *The Comprehensive Experiment*, Lewes, Falmer Press.

SHARP, A. (1981) 'The significance of classroom dissent', *Scottish Educational Review*, **13**, 2, pp.141–51.

TATTUM, D. (1982) *Disruptive Pupils in Schools and Units*, London, John Wiley.

TOPPING, K. (1983) *Educational Systems for Disruptive Adolescents*, London, Croom Helm.

WATKINS, C. and WAGNER, P. (1987) *School Discipline: A Whole School Approach*, Oxford, Basil Blackwell.

WILLIS, P. (1977) *Learning to Labour*, Farnborough, Saxon House.

WRAGG, E.C. (1993) *Primary Teaching Skills*, London, Routledge.

# Chapter 3

# Children Evaluating and Assessing Their Progress in Learning

*Hilary Emery*

## Why Should We Involve Children in the Assessment Process?

Teachers in the last few years have suffered from a barrage of information and requirements for assessment. Many feel that assessment has taken them away from their main purpose, namely teaching in the classroom. This chapter sets out to look at what is practical, manageable and useful in children being involved in the assessment process that will enhance their learning and the quality of teaching offered.

Teachers are drawn to examples of children's work as something that they find interesting. Of all the materials that were produced to support assessment between 1990 and 1993 the one category of publications from the School Examination and Assessment Council (SEAC) that was consistently welcomed as useful was the exemplification material: *Children's Work Assessed* for Key Stage 1 and *Pupils' Work Assessed* for Key Stage 3. In talking about these publications teachers mentioned the value of seeing pieces of children's work together with the context in which they were written so that they could make judgments about achievement. They also saw this as helpful in planning next steps in learning for the children.

In looking at such samples of children's work we find that the context is usually written by the teacher and the assessment decisions are made by the teacher. The child has generally not been involved in these decisions and may have a totally different impression of their work and progress. Some ten years ago this was brought home to me by a chance remark from Joanne, a cheerful Year-5 girl in my class. I saw her as intelligent, confident and very able at mathematics. Imagine my surprise when she remarked:

> You know Mrs Emery, Matthew is really good at maths. I'm just lucky that I get it right!

I was left with a sense of horror about equality of opportunity for both children, how far my perceptions differed from the child's and worst of all how I had managed to be unaware of her perception of her mathematical skills for so long. I had failed to find out how Joanne felt about her work and saw herself. While she saw herself as 'lucky', it was all too likely that she believed that one day the luck would run out. She did not have a valid perception of the strength of her mathematical understanding that she could use to help her in dealing with new and challenging mathematical problems. This started me looking at how children could be involved in assessing their learning to improve their perceptions of themselves as learners.

A couple of years later, as an advisory teacher, I found myself working with groups of teachers looking at assessment and talking about assessing a 'child's performance'. I was struck by the connotations associated with the word 'performance'. Collins English dictionary (1986) defines 'perform' as 'to fulfil or comply with' and goes on to define 'performance' as 'the act, process or art of performing'. This definition suggests the child's role in the learning process is to react to requirements set out by the teacher. It does not suggest an active part for children to play in their learning.

When set alongside research into the way children learn this worried me because there seemed no way, if children were only to perform, that they could show the teacher what they knew or where they were in their understanding. So I was faced with a challenge in the classroom — how was I to find out more about the way children saw themselves so that I could identify where they were in their understanding and in their perceptions of themselves as learners?

Of course this personal voyage of discovery was not unique. Many other teachers had been looking at these sorts of issues in both primary and secondary schools and finding ways to involve children in the assessment process. In secondary schools this led to the rapid expansion in the use of records of achievement during the 1980s and the implementation of a National Record of Achievement in the 1990s. Teachers had found that involving children in the assessment process encouraged them to become more active participants in their learning. This showed in higher levels of motivation and greater awareness of the range of their achievements: both academic and ones that went beyond the classroom.

In answer to the question: Why should I encourage children to evaluate and assess their own progress? the answers are about producing more effective learning, because children can be clearer about what they are being asked to do and how far they have achieved what they were asked to do. It should also help them to be aware of what they have done well, where they need to do more work and the sort of help they need to improve in that particular aspect. It fosters an atmosphere in which children can express their understanding of what is being taught and so aid the teacher to plan the learning experiences that will take this forward.

### This All Sounds Lovely in an Ideal World but How Do You Manage It in Practice?

This is the cry that rightly teachers come up with time and again and if pupil self-assessment is to become part of day-to-day practice we must address the issues of manageability and organization. Actively involving children in assessing their learning is something that some teachers have been doing for many years as part of good practice in the primary school.

In planning work on a day-to-day basis teachers have learning outcomes in mind that they anticipate the children will achieve during the lesson. One problem of manageability of assessment is getting round all the children to check that these outcomes have been achieved and by whom. A heartfelt cry from some trainee teachers wanting to develop their assessment strategies is 'Well I could do this sort of thing if I had an NTA in my classroom.' The underlying issue here is that this is one more additional task that the busy teacher alone may find there is insufficient time to undertake. Therefore to make pupil self-assessment manageable it needs to become an integral part of normal classroom life. The process might be:

- **Stage one**: In teaching you set out clearly to the children the learning outcomes that you expect and what you will be looking for in their work.
- **Stage two**: You ask the children to look out for these things as they work, so that when you come and talk to them as they are working they are able to tell you how they are getting on and you can help them see where they are on target and support them where they are having difficulties — possibly modifying expectations for some individuals. Abler children may need more challenging expectations set.
- **Stage three**: In marking children's work you refer to these learning outcomes in giving feedback and you group children together as far as possible to talk about the achievement of the overall learning outcomes. In addition you ask children to start to set individual, specific targets for themselves for the next week.
- **Stage four**: You plan to review these individual targets in ways that do not need you all the time, such as children using written self-assessment sheets, reviewing one another's work and giving parents an opportunity to add comments.

In stage one, by developing children's self-assessment skills teachers can involve the children in checking that their learning intentions are being achieved by sharing these intentions with them at the start of the lesson. In this way, as the children's skills are developed time can actually be released to focus the teaching more specifically on children's needs. In one large primary school teachers set out their intentions on the board at the start of the lesson and ask children to comment on the achievement of these in their written work when appropriate.

In getting children to comment on their own progress (stage two) some teachers feel that children will not be reliable in making judgments about their own progress in relation to the learning intentions. In practice sometimes children see their achievements as of a lower standard than teachers perceive and initially find self-assessment quite difficult (Barrs and Johnson, 1993; Dann, 1991). By making the differences in perception explicit the teacher can now address them and help the children to get a more accurate picture of their progress. This offers a significant step in developing their sense of self-esteem and also in helping them to see themselves as successful.

A few children may see themselves as better than the teacher perceives them to be. If they are doing this then it is likely that they would go on doing so in their heads anyway, and again the teacher has a chance to address their misconceptions and to decide why they hold them and how they can be addressed.

Giving children feedback on their work (stage three) raises problems of finding the time and managing the rest of the class. The videos *Communicating Progress* (TVS, 1992) and *Work In Progress* (TVS, 1991) show teachers developing pupils' self-assessment through termly individual reviews of their work and setting targets. By the nature of video work this gives a sample of what happens and teachers often feel it is somewhat idealized and the children shown seem to produce high standards of work while the rest of the class never come and interrupt the teacher doing the review. In reality things often seem rather different and if self-assessment is to be developed as a part of normal practice we need to recognize this reality.

Many teachers would like to talk to children about their work and review their progress on a regular basis but find it hard to organize the time. For example, to spend ten minutes with each child, each term, talking on a one-to-one basis would need about six hours a term for the average sized class. Where does that time come from and what do the rest of the class do, while this is happening, that is worthwhile?

The first part of the chapter sets out reasons for seeing the child as an active participant in the learning process of which assessment is an integral part. In practice with older children there are many occasions where they are able to review their work using a written form of response that they and the teacher may discuss individually or even in small groups after the teacher has had time to read and perhaps to sort out common issues that arise in children's written self-assessments. For younger children the question is whether teachers look for separate time to review or whether it is something that is done as an integral part of the normal pupil–teacher interactions during the day. If we tease this out, we find that the organized once a term review sessions set targets that might not be returned to until the following term. However, if such targets are realistic and achievable then in fact they need to be encouraged on a day-to-day basis and noted once they are achieved, so that new targets can be set as a normal part of day-to-day work.

I can hear the groans already as teachers anticipate that I am saying that they might need to review on a day-by-day basis. If teachers and children are setting targets as part of their normal dialogue about the work when teachers give back work or when talking with children as they are working, then they do not need a *separate* review time at all. This starts to offer a model for organizing children self-assessing and reviewing their progress that might be manageable.

As children are setting new learning targets for themselves regularly, teachers need to be able to record what these are, how children will know they have been achieved and when this has happened. If this takes the form of a public record, such as a classroom list, then there are opportunities for all the children to take some responsibility in helping one another to achieve their goals and to see how far they have got towards them. None of this needs the teacher to set aside ten minutes while the rest wait, patiently or not!

By identifying times when the children can look at, and assess, one another's work this can free the teacher to focus her teaching on children's needs. In my own classroom with Year 4 and 5 children this was used successfully when they completed major pieces of work such as a termly topic or the follow up to a school visit. The children had a deadline date for completion of the work and a specific time for assessing it together. I would introduce the assessment by asking them to decide the sort of things we should look for in commenting on the completed work. I then set these out on the board as a reminder for the children as they were looking at the work. We talked about what sort of comments would be helpful. We discussed how they did not like people saying nasty things about their work, but that if there was something that could have been done better they needed to say what they thought was wrong and how it could be improved next time e.g., 'This was hard to read because you had not checked the spelling and the writing was messy in places. Next time you could try using the computer to write some of the pieces.' I encouraged them to say why they made their comments e.g., 'I thought this was a good piece because you had used a lot of books to find out more about Queen Elizabeth.' Usually I would ask each child to look at three or four other books and put their comments on a sheet of paper at the back of the work. Children were encouraged to base their comments on evidence and present them in a constructive manner.

In developing this approach over the year the children began to have two types of criteria that they wanted to comment on. Initially, comments related to the overall standard of the work, but as the year progressed several children started to include comments about how well individual children had done because 'if you have worked hard and done it really well for *you* we should say so.'

No class of children is perfect and not every child on every occasion put the sort of comments that I might have wished. There were things such as 'I liked it.' 'Tis was rubbish.' (sic), but there were also comments like 'You tried really hard with your maps they look really good and you can see the way the Armada came to England.' They enjoyed seeing one another's work, they valued the comments of their peers and at times they took to heart and acted on the criticism of their peers more readily than if those comments had come from me.

A further strategy to make pupil self-assessment valuable in the classroom is to involve the parents. Teachers need to develop opportunities for parents to become involved in the assessment process as a normal part of the weekly or monthly routines. In one school children wrote about major pieces of work on a comments' sheet. They then took it and the sheet home for the parents to add a comment. The work included extended pieces of writing and problem solving in maths and science investigations that the children had developed for themselves.

Parents need to be clear what they are being asked to do and if teachers are going to involve them in the assessment process they need to give them some help and support to undertake it successfully. In practice this may need a parents' meeting to introduce the idea but it also needs some guidance on the piece of paper that parents write on, e.g., 'When you have had a look at the work and talked about your child's comments on the work please could you add a comment about an aspect you feel has been done well or that you were especially interested in.' It does not invite negative comments. The teachers encouraged parents who had concerns about the child's work to come and see them personally.

### Well Maybe I Could Find Some Time but Where Do I Start and What Should I Do? I'm Quite Sure You Can't Do that Sort of Thing with My Class!

Getting started is often the hardest part because we are talking about changing the culture of the classroom if this is really going to work. When I first started to encourage children to make comments about their own work they wanted to set large, rather vague targets such as 'I will stop getting so many spelling mistakes.' or 'I will write neatly.' Their comments were often concerned with presentation. The first step was to encourage children to refine these global statements into more specific and achievable statements such as 'I will read my work through when I finish to check the spellings.' or 'I will make all the tall letters go higher than the ordinary ones.'

As children got more used to assessing their work, being asked their opinions and being clear about expectations for the work, they began to refine the targets that they set for themselves. Increasingly their comments related to the content of the work or their skills in carrying it out e.g., 'I will make sure that I check my measurements in science before I write them down.' or 'I will write my next story so that there is a real ending not just "and I went to bed"'.

I suggested in the previous section, for manageability reasons and to support self-assessment as an integral part of teaching and learning, that teachers need to try and make the review of work a part of the normal routine. So, as teachers mark work they refer back to the purposes of the lesson that were set out or the learning objectives that were shared with the children and say how well they have achieved in relation to these. Sometimes we may say that we are interested in one thing but by the way in which we respond to the child's work we may actually show that it is something else about which we are really concerned e.g., presentation. We may suggest that we are concerned with the use of interesting language in their writing of a piece of creative poetry but all the marking on the first draft of the work may be in picking up spelling errors in unfamiliar and adventurous words and no comment on the way in which these have been used to express feelings or events. If we are looking for presentation as one of the criteria in assessing the work we need to say so to children; if not, it should not distract us from the criteria we have set out. This is not to say that if the child's presentation is poor it may be something to focus on in subsequent work, or in the example above on one of the later drafts.

As teachers move around the classroom commenting on children's work, they can refer to the purposes of the lesson and ask children their views on how well they feel they have been able to tackle the work. This helps to give a further insight into their current stage of learning. The change here may be that teachers spend no more time with each individual child than before but the teacher talks less and listens more as children explain how they see themselves progressing rather than the other way around. At the school where the teachers set out the purposes of their teaching at the start of each lesson they ask the children to comment afterwards on how well they think they have done the work.

In this way children are taking a more responsible role in the learning process and the teacher is showing that the child's views are valued and significant. Children may set learning targets that are listed publicly against which they can record progress for themselves and support one another in achieving them. They can be encouraged to show the teacher when these have been achieved. Initially this will not happen on its own and teachers will want to help children recognize where they have started to achieve their targets or to prompt them to be aware of them. As this way of working develops over a term the children will increasingly be able to do this for themselves and for one another.

If teachers want to develop formal review times for each child, they need to find times when the rest of the children are working and will not normally interrupt. One such time is silent reading but this may not fit with other policies on how this time should be used. Another way is to encourage all the children to review their work once a week at a certain time, for perhaps a quarter of an hour before lunch one day a week. They can discuss their work with one another and write their weekly reviews. At the same time the teacher can talk to individual children, perhaps talking to one or two children each week.

This is a strategy that means that all the children get a time with the teacher when the rest are involved in a similar process. Teachers may wish to encourage some peer reviews at this time as the children become more confident in self-assessment. This uses the time to best effect as the children review their previous targets, set new ones and comment on the week's work. One trainee teacher who took this approach found that the children's review sheets took a lot of time to read each week, but they told him so much that helped him in planning the next week that he sustained the approach through-out his final school experience.

Many teachers have developed very successful self-assessment sheets for children to record their comments. The CCW/WJEC Recording Achievement in Primary Schools project generated a lot of exciting examples of ways in which children commented upon their work two such examples are included here (Figures 3.1 and 3.2).

It is important that this sort of self-assessment is not overdone, otherwise teachers are likely to get to the equivalent of the apocryphal school trip comment: 'Don't touch it or you'll have to write about it!' Equally it should not be such a novelty that children do not develop their skills from one occasion to the next.

At the start of a new school year or when teachers first want to develop children's skills in self-assessment they may find it valuable to do some work on the children's perceptions of themselves. I have included a few examples of these as illustrations of the ways teachers can access children's perceptions of themselves (see Figures 3.3 to 3.6).

Figure 3.1:   Topic evaluation

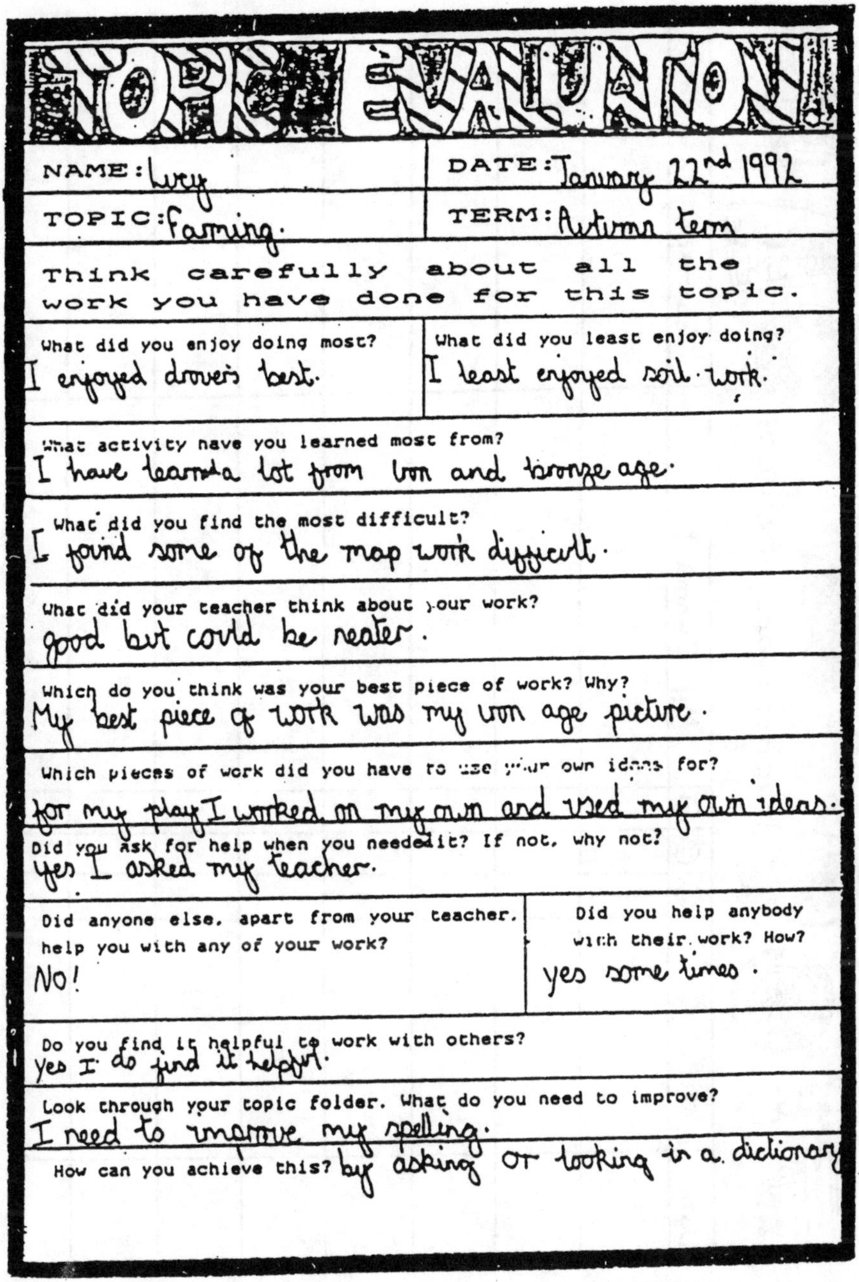

> **TOPIC EVALUATION**
>
> NAME: Lucy
> DATE: January 22nd 1992
> TOPIC: Faming.
> TERM: Autumn term
>
> **Think carefully about all the work you have done for this topic.**
>
> What did you enjoy doing most?
> I enjoyed droves best.
>
> What did you least enjoy doing?
> I least enjoyed soil work.
>
> What activity have you learned most from?
> I have learnt a lot from Iron and bronze age.
>
> What did you find the most difficult?
> I found some of the map work difficult.
>
> What did your teacher think about your work?
> good but could be neater.
>
> Which do you think was your best piece of work? Why?
> My best piece of work was my Iron age picture.
>
> Which pieces of work did you have to use your own ideas for?
> for my play I worked on my own and used my own ideas.
>
> Did you ask for help when you needed it? If not, why not?
> yes I asked my teacher.
>
> Did anyone else, apart from your teacher, help you with any of your work?
> No!
>
> Did you help anybody with their work? How?
> yes some times.
>
> Do you find it helpful to work with others?
> yes I do find it helpful.
>
> Look through your topic folder. What do you need to improve?
> I need to improve my spelling.
>
> How can you achieve this? by asking or looking in a dictionary

This sort of self assessment can be used in a generic manner for a variety of themes or topics.

Figure 3.2: *Invaders and settlers*

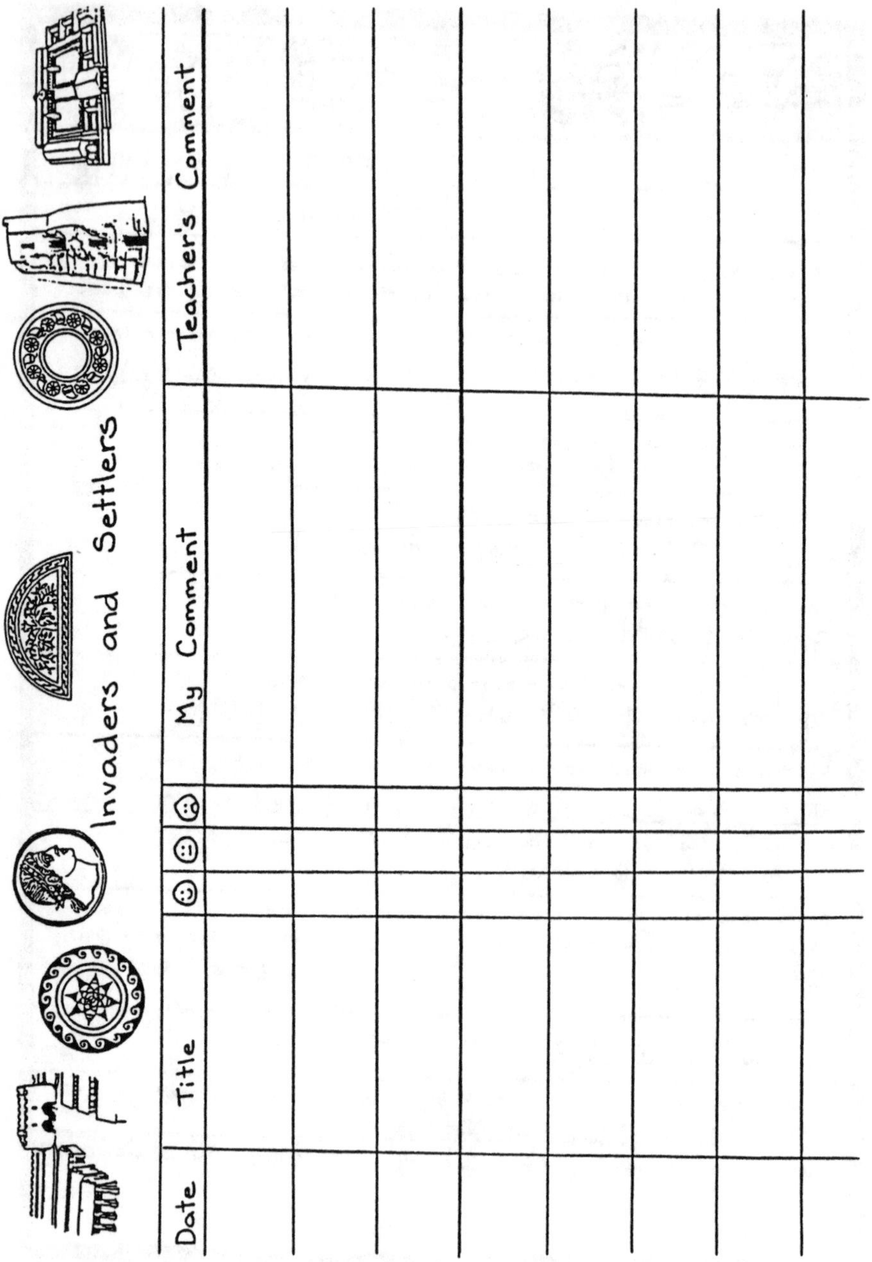

Invaders and Settlers

| Date | Title | ☺ | ☺ | ☺ | My Comment | Teacher's Comment |
|------|-------|---|---|---|------------|-------------------|
|      |       |   |   |   |            |                   |

This approach relates to a particular theme in history and allows specific items of work to be evaluated by both the teacher and the child.

Figure 3.3a:   Report on Robert

| Name | Robert | D.O.B | Class |
|---|---|---|---|
| Social Physical | Robert is tall and has blond hair and also he can be silly and he has good drawing skills and has five friends and good maths skills. He likes topic work he gets on with other children. And he's good at language. And he likes offertsking together | | |
| Maths | He has some good maths skills but. He does copy sometimes, He's not to good at tables but can be good at Baseword and he likes working in groups and and he can be very good at Nuffield but he likes doing. Logic and is good at it. | | |
| Language | He's very good at his spelling he is in red group but he not to good at english but he can be a bit good at it. He likes a lot of reading at reading time. He also likes slowget. in the way | | |
| Topic | He likes his topic work he likes animal topic the the best. He finished his time topic work from colors the doing with mrs Stuibbrungton and he's doing very well on it he. Did like on Holidays. | | |
| P.e. | He likes games the most but he can do sequencing not to good also the are scovers it the are tablevests it likes Aerobics too. and he likes dancing is the best. | | |

*Figure 3.3b:* Report on Tommy

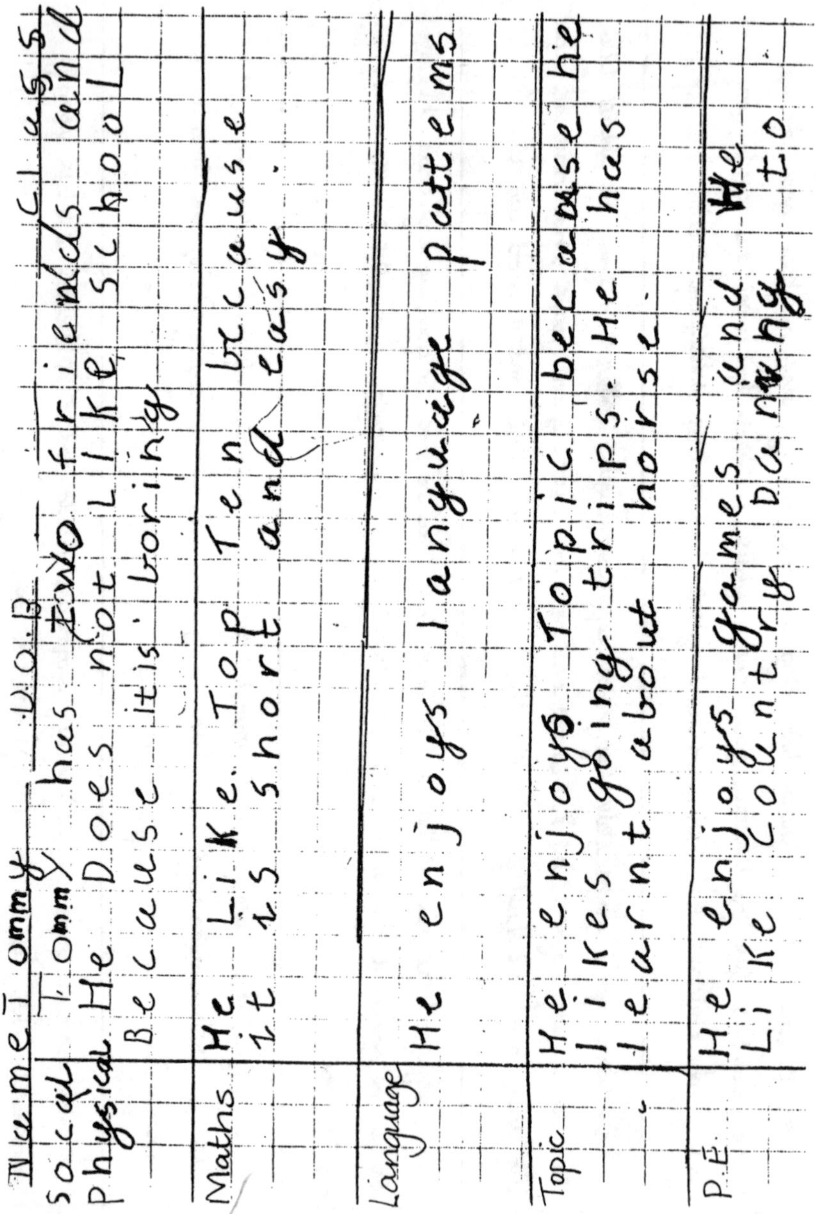

Name Tommy D.O.B

Social: Tommy has two friends class

Physical: He Does not Like school and Because it is boring

Maths: He Like Top Ten because it is short and easy.

Language: He enjoys language pattems

Topic: He enjoys Topic becase he likes going trips. He has learnt about horse.

P.E.: He enjoys games and He Like country Dancing to

These reports were written by year 6 children after talking about what reports contain, the sections that they could be divided into and the style of writing used. They gave some fascinating insights into these children at the mid-point of the year!

*Figure 3.4a: SEN example 1*

Figure 3.4b: SEN example 2

These two versions of the same sheet were used by a teacher of children with learning difficulties. She wanted all the children to have access to the task even if they were having reading difficulties.

*Figure 3.5: Personal growth banner*

**Key to personal growth banner**

1   My name
2   My four most cherished values in life
3   A personal motto which I try to live by
4   My three priority life goals
5   Three things I do well
6   Three areas that I wish to improve in
7   Three qualities that describe me

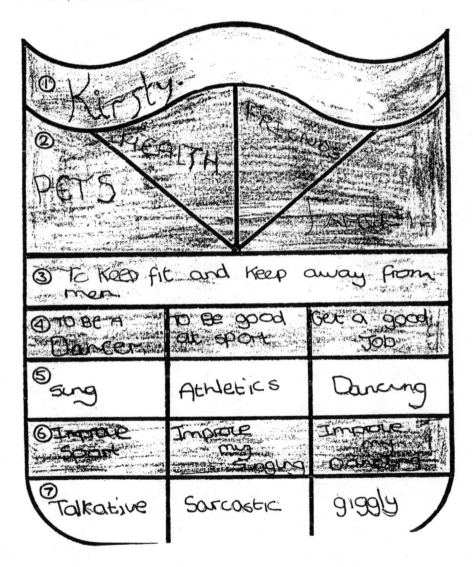

This example gives a vivid picture of a Year-7 pupil starting at secondary school.

*Hilary Emery*

Figure 3.6: *What am I like? How good am I at:?*

| WHAT AM I LIKE? | | HOW GOOD AM I AT:? | |
|---|---|---|---|
| Write a number in the box:<br><br>5 means - *Yes, that's me.*<br>4 means - *Yes, that's me most of the time.*<br>3 means - *Well, sometimes*<br>2 means - *Not very often*<br>1 means - *No, that's not me at all.* | | Write a number in the box:<br><br>5 means - *Very good*<br>4 means - *Good*<br>3 means - *OK*<br>2 means - *Not too good*<br>1 means - *Very poor* | |
| Neat and tidy | 4 | Dancing | 1 |
| Sensitive | 2 | Singing | 5 |
| Patient | 5 | Keeping a secret | 5 |
| Helpful to people | 4 | Sport | 5 |
| Careful | 5 | Reading | 5 |
| Thoughtful | 4 | Telling jokes | 4 |
| Hardworking | 5 | Getting up in the morning | 2 |
| Good with my hands | 3 | Talking | 5 |
| Restless | 4 | Listening | 4 |
| Easy going | 2 | Enjoying myself | 5 |
| Keen to do well | 5 | Working | 6 |
| Generous | 4 | Choosing clothes | 4 |
| Determined | 3 | Making friends | 4 |
| Talkative | 3 | Saving money | 3 |
| Kind | 4 | Remembering things | 4 |
| Like to be alone | 2 | Smiling | 5 |
| Trusting | 4 | Helping others | 5 |
| Keen to learn | 5 | Making people laugh | 4 |
| Strong | 4 | Getting what I want | 2 |
| Cheerful | 5 | Saying sorry | 5 |
| Happy | 4 | Winning | 4 |
| Shy | 2 | | |
| Brainy | 5 | | |
| My Name: Jonothan. | ....................................................... | | |

I included this example as a health warning of how careful we need
to be in interpreting the evidence that we are given. Jonothan who
completed this example is a thoughtful and considerate Year-3 child.
I was surprised that he had put only a rating of 2 (meaning not very
often) for sensitivity. When I asked him about this he said 'Well I
don't get upset very easily do I!' We need to be sure we are all using
the same interpretation and meaning for the words that we use!

To consolidate day-to-day self-assessment reviews some schools have developed a termly or annual review. The teacher goes through with the children their portfolios of work to select samples that are now out of date and send these home and to look at how well the samples that are kept reflect progress for each child. This review could be done as part of a parents' evening which might or might not include the child. Some schools have moved away from individual portfolios with the development of the National Curriculum assessment requirements. I would suggest that there remains a key role for individual portfolios so long as considerations of manageability and usefulness are kept in mind.

By looking through the portfolio children can be helped to see how their progress has emerged during an extended period of time. Sometimes this can raise conflicts between what a teacher and a pupil may wish to retain. This occurred for one teacher who had a child who felt that some of this work from earlier in the year was not very good and did not wish to keep it. The teacher considered that it was useful in indicating development and found the only way to resolve this was to agree with the child that she would keep these samples in a brown envelope at the back of the portfolio.

### How Do Children's Self-assessments Help Me When I Am Trying to Carry Out My National Curriculum Assessment of Level Descriptions?

Pupil self-assessment can contribute significantly to the assessment of level descriptions. Since level descriptions are intended to be used at the end of the key stage, on a day-to-day basis teachers need to assess in relation to the learning outcomes that they set. These are set in relation to their curriculum planning that derives from the whole school plan fleshed out in relation to the needs and abilities of the children in the class. The whole school plans relate to the programmes of study and so teachers ensure that the National Curriculum is being delivered. However they are also taking account of the individual children in each class and how well they are able to tackle the planned curriculum.

By involving the children in assessing themselves in relation to explicit shared learning objectives and outcomes the teacher gains more evidence from which to develop a reliable picture of each child's progress, inform future learning plans (formative teacher assessment) as well as discussions with parents and summative assessment in relation to the level descriptions at the end of the key stage. In this way as well as enhancing learning, motivation and self-esteem, pupil self-assessment can support the statutory assessment requirements.[1]

### Well You Convinced Me to Try a Couple of Things but Where Do I Go from Here?

Many teachers try these ideas and like the results and want to extend and sustain the approach. They want to integrate self-assessment to offer opportunities for the children to recognize their achievements and to set targets as a normal, integral part of their work.

To extend this work by individual teachers there is a need to consider pupil self-assessment at a whole school level. It implies for some teachers quite a cultural shift in the classroom if pupil evaluation and self-assessment are to be an integral part of normal teaching. This can have implications for teaching styles. Pupil self-assessment can then permeate all the work in the classroom and across the school.

In some schools this started through the work of one teacher that led to improvements in learning and motivation for the specific class. The teacher concerned then brought examples of self-assessments to discuss with the whole staff and consider how others could get started. For some teachers this can be quite threatening and there needs to be some sensitive support and encouragement, especially in the early stages when children are unfamiliar with what they are being asked to do and inevitably go through a learning stage themselves. One approach that I have found quite non-threatening is the report writing exercise shown above which is self-contained, fun, and offers some interesting children's work to bring back to a staff meeting for discussion. In other schools it has been a whole school commitment from the beginning as an integral part of the school's assessment policy. Whichever approach is taken to development the keys to success are to keep in mind that the intention is to offer something that is manageable and useful and enhances the quality of teaching and learning on offer.

## Note

1  My thanks go to Margaret Williams and Malcolm Bowring (1993) for the use of Lucy's topic evaluation; to teachers from a number of Hampshire schools who worked on the school based secondment programme in 1990/91 and to Weyford Junior School, Hampshire for other examples of children's assessments of their progress, as well as to children from classes that I have taught.

## References

BARRS, M. and JOHNSON, G. (1993) *Record Keeping in the Primary School*, London, Hodder and Stoughton.

DANN, R.C. (1991) Pupil assessment in the primary school: With special reference to the assessment implications of the Education Reform Act 1988, PhD thesis, University of Southampton.

HANKS, P. (Ed) (1986) *The Collins English Dictionary*, 2nd ed, London, W. Collins and Co.

SCHOOL EXAMINATION AND ASSESSMENT COUNCIL (1991) *Children's Work Assessed*, London, SEAC.

SCHOOL EXAMINATION AND ASSESSMENT COUNCIL (1992) *Pupil's Work Assessed*, London, SEAC.

TVS VIDEO (1991) *Work in Progress*, Southampton, Television South.

TVS VIDEO (1992) *Communicating Progress*, Southampton, Television South.

WILLIAMS, M. and BOWRING, M. (1993) *Records of Achievement in Primary Schools* (a development and support pack for schools) Cardiff, Curriculum Council for Wales and Welsh Joint Examination Council.

*Chapter 4*

# English Language Development Across the Curriculum in Multilingual Primary Classrooms

*Lynne Cameron*

The context of this chapter is the multilingual classroom, and the central concern is with the development of English language skills, mainly oral, across the curriculum. The pupils in such a classroom may have a range of first or home languages and will be at different stages in their learning of English, from beginners, who still say very little but understand some of what is said, to those who understand most of what they hear or read and who can usually express what they want to say in English. Some may be literate in their first languages, others will become literate first in English. In many British contexts, especially in northern urban areas, the geographical isolation of certain ethnic groups (as reported in the recent *Population Trends* survey (Owen, 1994)) means that most of the pupils' exposure to English will happen during the school day and within the classroom, with the teacher as major source of input. All the pupils, however, follow the same National Curriculum, and the teacher has the dual role of making the curriculum content accessible to all the pupils and of developing English language skills.

Teachers of such classes have a great advantage if they speak the first language(s) of the children fluently, and are thus able to understand children's questions and responses, to get across difficult concepts through the more familiar language first, to reassure children when they are ill or just confused. This scenario is unfortunately quite rare in Britain. More likely, the teacher will be monolingual, perhaps with a bilingual assistant or nursery nurse, and with the school or authority language support team providing regular, but not necessarily frequent, help in planning work and in teaching bilingual pupils.

Whether or not the teacher is bilingual, developing children's English language skills through curriculum activities requires an understanding of what those skills are, and an understanding of progression in the mastery of those skills. In the early and mid-1980s when special language centres which provided English language tuition to newly arrived immigrant pupils were being closed down and all bilingual children were placed in mainstream classrooms, it was sometimes argued that the rich environment of the primary classroom would provide a natural language learning context, and little extra help would be required. Experience since that time shows that we should not underestimate the task of pupils and teachers in developing language skills while at the same time learning content. Learning and operating in a new language is an experience involving the whole child, touching, and sometimes threatening, the heart of identity and self-esteem. It needs to take place in a supportive environment where the child's language and cultural background are valued and respected, and for many reasons the mainstream classroom is the only possible location. At the same time, existing methodology is not always successful; it is not uncommon for secondary teachers to claim that their bilingual pupils seem not to know basic subject vocabulary, or cannot put together more than a few words in response to questions, and the lack of achievement in public examinations in certain schools nationally reflects the failure of some pupils to reach their potential in both English language and the subjects they study through English. We need to know much more than we do currently about language in the education of bilingual pupils, but while waiting for such research to be done, a useful working principle would seem to be that, as teachers and as trainers, the more we understand about language and language learning, the more we will understand about what goes to make successful classroom pedagogy and educational policy.

In this chapter, therefore, I aim to outline one way of describing the process of English language development in multilingual classroom contexts, in the belief that precision in description and thinking about language issues is not opposed to currently fashionable 'whole language' approaches. Rather, a teacher's knowledge about language can profitably combine with holistic educational aims in the planning and implementation of classroom activities across the curriculum which will help promote language skills development.

I start by putting the multilingual classroom into an international perspective from which to view current provision in Britain, and to highlight issues and possibilities for action within the constraints of that provision. I then draw on research into language and language learning in order to suggest key principles for promoting English language development across the curriculum. Finally, I make some concrete suggestions for classroom teachers and language coordinators on how to become more 'language aware' or 'language sensitive' in teaching and planning.

## International Perspectives on Learning through a Second Language

In this section I'd like to give an international perspective to the phenomenon of children learning through a language that is different from the one they use at home. Britain, in particular England, since bilingual education is available in Wales, does not emerge very well from such a viewpoint. There is very little

UK research into the effects of bilingualism or of instruction in English, with educational decisions about planning and delivery of second language education often apparently made on the basis of political and financial expediency rather than on educational benefits for the learners.

It is in fact common around the world to find classrooms in which children are operating in a language that is not their first language, and common too for that second language to be English. In many subSaharan African countries, a national language different from most children's first languages is used as the medium of primary education — Swahili in Tanzania, Portuguese in Mozambique, English or Afrikaans in South Africa. In addition, English is often introduced as a subject in primary school, prior to becoming the medium of instruction in secondary schools. In multi-ethnic Malaysia, the national language Bahasa Melayu, which is the second language of many children, is used in most primary schools. In the United States, Spanish-speaking Latino children attend English-speaking schools and kindergartens, while some states offer immersion education in Spanish or French for English-speaking children. In bilingual Canada, French-speaking children can enrol in immersion programmes in English-speaking schools, and vice versa. In the Netherlands, Turkish-speaking children learn through Dutch; in European Schools in Belgium and other countries, children learn through their first languages and later study part of the curriculum through their second or third languages; the list could be continued across Europe and Asia across socio-economic classes and ethnic groups.

Not all these educational systems are equally successful — Latino students in US schools appear to underachieve (Lucas, Henze and Donato, 1990), while immersion programmes in Canada record successful learning of both language and content (e.g., Swain and Lapkin, 1982). Even within one system, indeed one school, the differential success of, say, Bosnian refugees and some British Asian children can be surprising. What appear to be the causes for differences in achievement and can they give us any useful information as to how to provide the best possible learning environment for British bilingual children?

The picture that emerges is complex, with decisions about language in education as one factor among many other interdependent factors: social, economic, cultural and political. It is possible to start from any one, or any combination, of these factors and trace potential causes of success and failure in education. What is more, since examination of many of the issues is inevitably controversial, both the selection of starting point and methods of investigation are open to attack on ideological grounds. As an illustration close to home, we can recall the heated debates over including spoken Standard English in the National Curriculum, a relatively uncontroversial issue compared to, for example, the imposition of Afrikaans education on black South Africans or the bussing of black children in the southern United States. I would like to draw three issues of importance out of the complexity.

Firstly, when we discuss the education of bilingual children in any

context, the social, cultural, economic and political factors should not be neglected. We are educating children within particular social contexts that affect
every decision we make and every outcome we observe, and our decisions
and observations should take account of that. Working with bilingual children
provides endless opportunities for widening teachers' own cultural horizons
and revealing how language is structured by, and structures, our understanding of the world. One immediate result is that we begin to understand the
complexity of growing up bilingual, respecting and valuing what bilingual
children bring to their school experiences, rather than seeing them as deficient
English language users.

This relates to the second point I would like to draw from national and
international research — the importance of holding consistently high expectations of bilingual pupils and translating these into effective school and classroom practice. Expectations of success in school through application of both
teachers and pupils are demonstrated in the values and attitudes held by staff
and transmitted to pupils: respect for each other, and for each other's languages and cultures; expectation of cooperation within school and between
home and school in matters of information-giving, attendance, punctuality;
cognitively challenging work set for pupils to do in class, that is always completed, well-presented, and valued by pupils and teachers; children provided
with appropriate equipment and resources; minority group role models to
follow, preferably among the people who teach, but certainly among visitors
to the school.

The third point to be made is that the temptation to ignore the role of
language because of the ideological implications should be resisted. Bilingual
pupils in Britain do need English language skills in order to achieve academic-
ally and to have equal opportunities in our society, and we do therefore need
to develop better ways of teaching those skills. At the same time, it is clear
from the international perspective that educational success is more likely for
children who can begin their schooling in their first language, switching to the
second when a firm basis in both has been achieved, and continuing to develop skills, including literacy, in the first language. Such genuine bilingual
education, which develops each of a child's two languages, is much more
likely to be on offer to majority group children, e.g., English-speaking Canadians,
than to those from minority groups e.g., Panjabi-speaking British children.

The importance of first language development for academic success has
been established by the work of Cummins in Canada (see Cummins and Swain
(1986) for details), and has a direct link with the role and status of bilingual
teachers, classroom assistants or nursery nurses in British schools. Where this
bilingual expertise is used to support children's learning, and not merely to
translate a monolingual teacher's input, it can be of great benefit to children.
Much more work is needed to find out how best to make use of bilingual
teaching skills in the classroom and how to train all teachers to exploit the
possibilities.

*Lynne Cameron*

## Current National Policy on Second Language Education

Despite the evidence that developing children's first language skills can benefit all aspects of their learning, including second language skills, bilingual education, outside Wales, is not government policy. The 1994/95 revision of the National Curriculum for English recognizes the 'richness' of other languages, but sees them as useful towards the learning of English: 'pupils should be encouraged to make use of their understanding and skills in other languages when learning English' (DfE, 1994). Some schemes for introducing bilingual classroom assistants have been introduced, but in reality, bilingual education is less likely to be the aim of a school than the development of English language.

The history and practice of mainstreaming of bilingual children can be read in *Moving into the Mainstream* (Bourne, 1989). Currently, support for language development in mainstreaming comes from teachers funded by central government. These language support teachers work in teams, in schools where there are sufficient bilingual pupils to warrant it, or otherwise, in local authority teams, visiting schools with bilingual pupils on a rota basis. They provide two main types of support: access to curriculum for individual pupils, or whole-class and whole curriculum support by working with the class teacher in planning and delivery. Not all class teachers with bilingual pupils have access to support staff, and certainly not for major periods of the school day.

This level of provision of language support means in practice that the school, language coordinators and class teachers must take the responsibility for enabling access to the full curriculum for bilingual pupils, and for developing their English language skills. At school level, this should be formalized in a school policy on language, with, possibly, additional policy statements on the development of bilingualism, on equal opportunities, and on anti-racism. Guided by school policy and the National Curriculum Programmes of Study, the individual teacher then has the task of planning support for understanding of content and language development into daily classroom practice.

## English Language: Skills and Strands

As I move now into more detailed description of English and how it is used for different purposes in and out of school, it may be helpful to think of what happens in the primary classroom in terms of a series of *events*, designed and orchestrated by the teacher, experienced by the pupils and the teacher, and, in real time, jointly constructed by what teachers and pupils say and do. Examples of such classroom events would be: reading a story; taking the register; a maths activity set up and carried out by a small group; discussing a design brief with a partner. The events may have as their prime objective either learning in one or more curriculum areas, or the completion of some organizational or administrative task. Each classroom event involves the use of language by teacher and pupils to organize, to challenge thinking, to check understanding or for some other purposes, and each event has potential for language development. In order to take advantage of this potential, we need the tools to analyse and understand the way language is used in classroom events. Knowing about English gives a teacher terminology and concepts to use in planning, in intervention in learning, and in assessment. That's why in this section I want to take language, in particular English, apart, to see how it works and how children learn to use it. Once English language has been divided up in various ways I will proceed to show how skills can be developed.

To help my division of language make more sense, I will use an example taken from a recent OFSTED report on an infant school in Dewsbury, West Yorkshire (OFSTED, 1994), which found much excellent practice in the education of bilingual pupils. A sequence of activities, combining work from the National Curriculum Key Stage 1 Programmes of Study in geography, science, and design and technology, firstly involved the children in visiting a local shop to buy fruit. The different types of fruit were then investigated for their properties, and then made into *chaat* or fruit salad. The report gives no further information on what was done, but I will, in what follows, explore some of the language development possibilities of such activities.

The first separation that can help thinking and planning is to be made between concepts and the particular language in which they are expressed. Conceptual knowledge, labelled 'common underlying proficiency' by Cummins (1984), can be expressed in any of the languages that a child speaks. Concepts are easiest acquired in the most familiar language of the child, and can be transferred into the second language once the language elements are known. When children have to learn both new concepts and new language, they will need more time and more support for meaning, provided through concrete objects, first-hand experience, pictures, diagrams, gestures, or through translation into their first language. In the fruit investigation, we can see that children are likely to have conceptual understanding of, say, 'sweet' and 'sour', but may not have the language to express it in English, or in their first language. More abstract or complex concepts, such as the biological differences between fruits, nuts and seeds (Key Stage 2), will be more difficult to grasp, and will require language to explain them, along with visual support. In this case, fairly simple language labels cognitively complex concepts. In planning for children's learning, the complexity of the conceptual knowledge objectives will affect the amount and type of support given to help pupils' understanding. In using activities and talk to develop understanding, the teacher needs to check both conceptual development and language comprehension. If a pupil does not understand something, the teacher needs to find out whether the concept is the problem or whether the problem lies in the language used to talk about the concept. A range of checking strategies for use when teaching content through English are given in Table 4.1.

A further importance of this separation of concepts and language lies in how it breaks down the umbrella term 'ability' as applied to bilingual pupils, reminding us of the need to distinguish the ease or difficulty with which a

Table 4.1: Strategies for checking pupils' understanding of language, content, and task

---

**Teacher taking responsibility for checking understanding**

- Using expected outcomes of tasks as evidence for pupils' understanding of the task instructions, content and language. This would require initial identification of which particular outcomes would constitute evidence of understanding.
- Giving pupils time to respond to checking questions i.e., pausing after asking them.
- Repeating a question in an identical form, or in a different form.
- Check pupils' understanding by getting them to produce examples of concepts explained by the teacher. They could tell their examples to the teacher, to the class, to a partner (which adds the opportunity to justify).
- Having the pupils show a partner how to do what they have been taught i.e., pass on a skill.
- Having the pupils test out ideas or preconceptions.
- Observing pupils' faces.
- Making concrete links with abstract ideas; involve the pupils physically in explaining concepts.
- Breaking down a demonstration/task into small steps and checking each step.
- Teacher asking pupils to re-articulate input — pupil tells teacher what teacher said.
- Teacher asking pupils about a particular aspect of information inputted (e.g., what will we have when we're finished?) or from a different point of view (put the information listened to on to a diagram/chart).
- Writing, or telling a partner, a summary of what has been read — with the book closed.

**Enabling pupils to take responsibility for checking**

- Talking explicitly about the learning potential of responding to teachers' questions and agreeing strategies together e.g., encouraging/requiring pupils to guess if they are not sure.
- Giving pupils time to prepare questions to ask the teacher or each other to check understanding or clarify.
- Exploiting or creating situations in which the pupil is the 'expert' and the teacher or other pupils need to ask for information. This would give practice in the answering and asking of questions.
- For their understanding of instructions — use written and graphic as well as oral instructions; use activities such as sequencing pictures that show the process, matching pictures with written instructions, using written instructions when completing the task.
- Directed reading: some pupils receive information e.g., on task instructions, that they then have to convey to others.
- Jigsaw tasks or instructions: Pupils collect information in one group, and are then regrouped to share that information with, and receive information from, others to end up with a complete set of information.
- As part of self-evaluation at the end of a task or lesson — 'Is there any part of the task I'm still not sure about?'

---

Note: This checklist was compiled in an in-service workshop with colleagues from the University of Leeds and teachers from a local school.

child acquires new concepts from the current level of the child's English language. Such a distinction should affect both assessment and the grouping of pupils within a class. Valid assessment of a child's understanding requires that we go beyond a child's possible limitations in English; if someone who speaks a child's first language is not available, then assessment of conceptual knowledge requires imaginative use of non-verbal techniques. The grouping or setting of children by 'ability' is fraught with the same difficulties (Bourne, 1994, p.220), and may also risk not setting expectations high enough; it may be better to use a range of ways of grouping, sometimes by language level, sometimes mixing language levels, so that children have a chance to learn from, and to help, others. In addition, bilingual children's English will be developing quickly but not consistently, and phases of rapid language growth may alternate with phases of little apparent development. Grouping by language level that seemed appropriate at the beginning of a term, may well seem less appropriate in the second half of the term.

Having established the need to be able to separate language from concepts encoded in language, a second key distinction is between receptive and productive skills, in oral language between listening and speaking skills in English. Although both types of skills are crucial (after all it is very hard to find a human communicative activity in which one is used without the other) we must not forget that a child who receptively understands something — for example, watching and listening to the teacher describing how to make a fruit salad — has probably not, through just listening, mastered the productive skills needed to describe the same process to somebody else. In fact, the child will need more listening, together with practice and encouragement in speaking, before the much more difficult production task can be performed. It is because the development of speaking skills, vital for children's academic achievement, is much more difficult than developing listening skills that this distinction is made here. As with the learning of other skills, from riding a bicycle to painting, motivated and meaningful practice of production skills is crucial — children need to speak in English in order to get better at speaking in English, and this means that as well as setting up tasks that involve children talking to each other, the teacher and other adults in the classroom have a key role as speaking partners for pupils.

Let's now break down productive/receptive language skills into further strands. The following categories describe language in ways useful for analysing language use and language development:

- vocabulary
- grammar $\Big\langle$ morphology  
  syntax
- phonology
- conversation
- extended discourse

Each of the above strands of language contains a range of possibilities from the very simple to the very complex, and may differ across different curriculum areas. Development within each strand needs specific planning and monitoring, and can be detailed within any one activity.

Each one is now described in more detail, with examples related to the fruit activities used to help clarify them.

## *Vocabulary*

Words of different types, and of different levels of complexity from basic to more specific or more general.

> e.g., *Nouns*: names of fruits and the parts of fruit apple, orange peel, pips, core, slices
> *Adjectives* to describe the fruit round, red, ripe, big, Spanish
> *Verbs* grow, germinate, cut, chop, slice, cube

In vocabulary learning, comprehension is much easier, especially when concrete examples or pictures can be used, than is production. In production, the appropriate word has to be found and recalled; it then has to be used correctly with other words.

## *Morphology*

The ways in which words change their shape for tense: chop*ped*, slice*d*; for number apple*s*; to agree with other words: I chop, she chop*s*.

Morphology has to be learnt both receptively and productively. In reception there are usually other clues to tense or number, through language or visuals. In production, though, accurate selection of word endings is the aim, and requires matching with other words in the same sentence.

## *Syntax*

Ways of combining words to express simple or more complex ideas.

> The orange is round and juicy.
> The orange is sweet but the lemon is sour.
> We put the orange in the bowl and then we added the apple.

Again, accuracy is needed to convey meanings in production. In reception, the logical links between key words can be worked out from other clues to meaning, and the grammatical patterns are less necessary. As the child moves through primary school, the information carried by the grammar becomes more crucial to the understanding of the precise meaning of what is heard or read.

## *Phonology*

The pronunciation of words, and the intonation and stress patterns of English. This is clearly a feature of production rather than reception.

*Conversation*

The skills needed to take part in conversation in English — for example, answering and posing questions; greeting and responding to greetings; initiating talk; taking turns at speaking. Such skills would be needed to:

talk to shopkeeper to find out prices / where fruit comes from
discuss with teacher and other pupils how best to make fruit salad.

In conversation, production and reception skills are combined; pupils who respond with single words or silence are showing that they have less confidence, and need to develop skills in production.

Conversations in the classroom have their own special rules that children have to work out. For example: We don't play games with knives do we? is a teacher question that is actually designed to discipline a child; and a pupil response received with a further question probably means the pupil gave an inappropriate answer:

**Teacher**   What's this?
**Pupil**   An apple.
**Teacher**   An apple? Are you sure?

*Extended Discourse*

The skills needed to talk or write at length. For example, to

describe how the ripeness of different fruits was tested.
explain to another child the process of preparing fruit for fruit salad.

This strand is the most demanding on language production skills, requiring a set of ideas to be logically linked together and expressed coherently and cohesively. Children need models, support and practice in producing extended discourse of different types across the curriculum e.g., for science, for stories, for solutions to mathematical problems. Such modelling and practice will probably be needed throughout primary school, and is appropriate often in first language skills development too.

*Literacy*

How English is written down, the relation between symbols, sounds and meanings.

Labels in the fruit shop of names and prices.
Reading the recipe and following it.
Writing a simple report of the process of making the fruit salad.

This strand of language can, of course, itself be further broken down to help in planning development. It is included here as a reminder of its cognitive demands and the need for specific teaching of literacy.

Some of the strands will need more attention than others, or specific attention at certain points; for example, children are renowned for their skill in acquiring the sounds and intonation of new languages and, helped by learning plenty of songs and rhymes, should not have too many problems. In other areas, such as morphology and syntax, there seem to be maturational constraints on development in first or second language that mean certain structures, such as relative clauses, will not be acquired until the later stages of primary school. The distinction between conversation and extended discourse is an important one, because each needs specific practice in order to develop the specific skills involved and we cannot assume that a child who can hold a conversation can also produce a longer piece of talk such as a description or explanation. Children are much quicker at acquiring conversational skills in a new language than they are at acquiring what Cummins (1984) calls 'academic skills', which include literacy and extended discourse of different types. His research has shown that children can speak in conversation as fluently as their peers after two years of learning English, but that it takes five to seven years to catch up with academic skills.

## Progression in Language Skills Development

Let's start with a description of the typical language development of a child learning English through his or her experiences in preschool and infant classrooms. Children who come into an English-speaking environment later in their primary education will probably pass through the same stages, but more quickly. It is not unusual for young children put into a new language context initially to say nothing at all, either in English or in their first language. The experience of not being able to make themselves understood to adults or other children, and of not understanding what is being said, is bewildering and puzzling, and while some children continue to use their first language, others stop trying to make themselves understood verbally. Non-verbal communication, pulling, gesturing and making noises, may be used for urgent needs. All this time though, the child is listening to the new language and trying to make sense of how it is used. Eventually, he or she will begin to use individual words, and groups of words or phrases which are learnt as whole chunks. These formulaic utterances seem to act as the scaffolding framework for language in the child's mind, with words being slotted in and the phrases being rearranged. So 'I want it' as a formula may be adapted in particular situations to 'I want it drink' or 'I want it go home'. Changes to formulae such as 'You want it drink?' show the child beginning to create the grammar of the language. The child gradually acquires more possible ways of putting words into sentences to express a wider range of communicative needs, along with a developing vocabulary of different types of words. The social skills of the new language are learnt at the same time: culturally determined ways of expressing politeness, finding out answers to questions, getting people to help. Although the child as language learner appears to develop on a broad front, mastering aspects of the new language holistically, attention to subcomponents can be seen in the constructive errors like 'bringed' for 'brought', and in the phase of asking for the English names for everything in sight.

The work of Snow and others (e.g., Snow, 1995) has shown that progress in the different strands identified in the last section depends too on the experience the child has with that aspect of language. So a child exposed to a wide range of words will acquire a wide vocabulary, and a child who experiences plenty of explanations and descriptions will develop good skills in extended discourse.

The most useful model of language learning that accounts for the kind of progression observed is one that has the learner actively building up in his or her brain a representation of how the language works and how the parts of the language relate to each other, and acquiring, through practice, a set of skills for using this language system. The learner constructs the language system internally through hearing the language used meaningfully (exposure), through subconsciously finding patterns and rules in what is heard and storing these patterns ready for later use in production. The patterns stored are simple at first, gradually becoming more complex to take account of new input. Using the language gives the learner opportunities to try out patterns and receive feedback as to whether they are understood or not. When forced to try and communicate without sufficient knowledge, the learner will have to use whatever is available and supplement it with pointing, with words in the first language. Alternatively, the learner may avoid communication altogether and go for simpler talk within existing knowledge.

The basic needs for language learning to take place in classrooms, from research in Canada and elsewhere (Lightbown and Spada, 1993), appear to include the following:

- exposure to the language;
- output: use of the language;
- corrective feedback: information about the success or failure of attempts to communicate; and
- focus on form: explicit attention to particular features of the language.

*Exposure*

Exposure or input seems so important for language learning that it has even been suggested that input would be enough without any output; more recent theory and research supports the idea that output (practice in using the language) is also crucial. The type of exposure affects the amount of learning; just watching television will not make children learn language, although children's programmes where meaning is very clear, as in cartoons, certainly help. The language children are exposed to must be within or just beyond their current understanding, with support for meaning from visual aids or context, use of repetition and redundancy (saying the same thing in different ways, building in more information than is absolutely necessary); it must be attended to in some way by the pupils and not be just background noise, which means it must be motivating and interesting. Teachers and classroom assistants can provide exposure for individuals by picking up topics in which they are interested and offering statements and questions to the child, in a similar way to how parents interact with younger children e.g.:

> You've got a plaster on your finger! Did you cut it? How did you do that? With a knife? Were you cutting something? Did you cry when you cut your finger? Has anyone else got a plaster? Oh yes, Indira's got a plaster on her finger, and John's got a plaster on his knee.

Children's responses to questions can be expanded, providing them with relevant and immediate input:

| **Teacher** | Look at this picture! |
| **Child** | bird tree. |
| **Teacher** | Yes. There's a bird in the tree. He's sitting on the branch. He's singing — look, his beak's open. |

For children from minority groups who seldom meet native speakers of English outside school, English language input provided in school is their only source and must therefore be maximized and maximally useful. The routines of classroom life — taking the register, lining up, collecting and giving out materials, story or news time — provide excellent opportunities for exposure to English where predictability and context assists understanding of the language, and where the grammatical forms and vocabulary can be repeated and as they are learned, made more complex.

### Output

I have mentioned the need for learners to use the language in order to learn it — the importance of output of different types and lengths. Again, school may be the only context in which some children are required to use English; care needs to be taken in setting tasks for children to ensure that they are required to use the English they have acquired. Too often, classroom events can proceed with children producing only single word responses to teacher questions or very simple instructions or commands to other pupils in order to get group work tasks completed.

*Corrective Feedback*

Corrective feedback can be seen as necessary information for learning, allowing the child to see when the system he or she has constructed needs further adjustment. The most common way to provide such feedback is by accepting a child's inaccurate phrase and offering it back in the correct form:

**Child**   My mummy hospital.
**Teacher**   Oh, your mummy went to hospital. Why?

*Focus on Form*

The most recent research shows that while children in immersion programmes become very fluent, their second language production is often inaccurate, with errors or gaps in different strands of language: for example, morphological errors in the choice of tenses, or in agreements between subject and verb; vocabulary gaps or inappropriate choices. Focusing on form involves the teacher in drawing the pupils' attention to specific language features and talking about them. Bilingual children have been shown to have a greater awareness about language and to be better at noticing facts about language than monolingual children, and so explicit attention to language details can build on these capabilities. I would suggest that such a focus could use ideas from 'Language Awareness' (see suggested resources) to help children think about English. Pupils can be encouraged to compare English with their first language(s); Bourne (1989) provides a nice example of pupils and bilingual assistant discussing whether 'egg' as applied to caterpillars and to birds would be translated by one word in Panjabi, or whether different words would be used. In the National Curriculum for English Programmes of Study, Section 3 of each Key Stage has detailed suggestions for aspects of English to be studied, and each Curriculum Subject makes references to aspects of language use in that subject area.

The older the child, the more conscious attention to, and reflection on, features of language will be possible and useful. Explicit discussion of language and language use enables pupils to build up autonomous language learning skills and to become learners who continue developing language. The other crucial factor in continued language learning is, of course, continuing motivation. A sense of achievement, linked to meeting high expectations, can help learning through the use of progressively more cognitively demanding topics, with increasingly complex input and output.

## Planning and Teaching for Language Development Across the Curriculum

In addition to general suggestions made already, this section offers more specific ideas for class teachers and language coordinators.

### Developing Your Background Knowledge

- Find out and increase your own knowledge of the language or languages your children use at home and in the community, and of the level of their skills in each of their languages. Your bilingual pupils are bringing into your classroom rich cultural and language resources that can be used to make the curriculum come alive for them, but only if you have the knowledge to do so. This information may already be in the school, gathered through home–school liaison work, or you may need to seek it out by talking with parents or older children.
- Try learning some words and phrases in the children's first language. This can have a double benefit: it helps to understand the different ways in which languages work in the different strands mentioned earlier, and being able to ask basic questions and to say some phrases may be useful in the classroom or with parents. Since a language and the way it is used are inextricably linked with culture, learning language can open up ways into culture.
- Find out too about your school language and/or anti-racist policy — what does it say about bilingual language development, about valuing different cultures and languages?
- If you are the language coordinator, set up a group to revise policies if necessary.
- Find out, and keep updated, information about the levels of English of your children — again the school may well have this information if children are tested at some point. Other information can be gained by talking to the children as they work or play, identifying gaps, and by trying out different groupings of children and observing outcomes.

### Valuing and Developing the First Language Skills of the Children

- Develop a school policy that encourages planned use of bilingual input to develop language and literacy skills in first language(s).
- Support the provision of examination classes in community languages in local secondary schools.
- Support community efforts to set up language classes.
- Encourage bilingual adults or older pupils on work experience to come into class and use the first language(s) for specific purposes, carefully planned with you in advance.

### Increase the Children's Useful Exposure to English

- Get English-speaking adults and older children into the classroom on a regular basis, and with a clear brief on how to talk to children as they play or work.
- Teach the children playground rhymes and songs in English.

- *Through Stories and Reading Aloud*

    - Choose stories to read that include repetition, predictable happenings, and good visuals to support the meaning.
    - Record stories as you tell them and let children borrow cassettes to listen to at home.
    - Read aloud other types of text to the children too: non-fiction of different sorts, poetry, newspaper items.
    - Keep parents informed about what their children are learning so they can support their children by listening to new songs, asking for numbers and colours in English, hearing their children read etc.
    - Have children's videos and cassettes on sale at school fairs and book clubs.
    - Practise seeing every event in the classroom as a potential opportunity for language development through input, output, feedback and explicit attention to language. When planning in advance, work out what language from each strand can be recycled and what new language can be introduced.

- *Through Teacher Talk*

The teacher talk that accompanies a classroom event is a vital source of input for children and benefits from being thought about carefully:

    - Plan the English you will use in setting up activities so that children understand the purpose and procedure.
    - Decide when it will be useful to model extended discourse. For example, when working with a small group of children on maths problems, you may explain the solution of a problem to them and then ask them to explain it back to you, or to explain a different problem in the same way to a partner; when working on hypothesizing or predicting, you can suggest one or two possibilities before asking the children to present theirs e.g., 'I think that the most expensive fruit will be the mango because it comes from far away', or, 'it might be the grapes because they're difficult to grow.'
    - Select questions that suit your purposes: closed questions with short answers are suitable for checking conceptual knowledge e.g., 'What are the seeds of an apple called?' open or higher-order questions encourage children to explore ideas through talk e.g., 'What do you think will happen next? why do more people like apples than like oranges?' These questions help develop language, but children will need more support in answering them, including more time to put together an answer.
    - At the end of an activity, use teacher talk to summarize what's been discovered and learnt.

- It can be very helpful to monitor your teacher talk by recording yourself, transcribing the tape and asking some questions about what you find: Is your talk understandable by the pupils it is aimed at? Does your talk stretch and challenge the children's language and thinking? Does your talk provide models and opportunities for children's talk?
- This kind of investigation can work well as in-service training, when a group of teachers get together to record and analyse, perhaps observing each other too.

### Planning for Output

- Ensure that each day provides opportunities for language production, both conversational and extended discourse, of different types, through pair work, small group work, and pupil–teacher talk.
- Plan for structured outcomes to activities — here is where accurate production of oral or written English can be given a purpose and an audience (children, other classes, parents and teachers). The fruit activities used earlier could provide the following examples of structured outcomes:
  - group posters showing the results of investigations into the properties of different fruits, presented to the class with a short commentary, recorded on tape to listen to later;
  - class or individual zig-zag books describing the visit to the shop in pictures and sentences, perhaps with photographs taken at the time;
  - individual copies of the fruit salad recipe in two languages for children to take home; and
  - giving a demonstration of making the fruit salad, with scripted commentary, to another class.
- The work of the National Oracy Project (Norman, 1992) provides many more ideas for developing talk with bilingual pupils.

## Conclusion

Increasing oral and literacy skills in two or more languages is part of the growing all-round competence of the bilingual child. Within the primary classroom, bilingual pupils need to be exploring and developing their skills in English, and the informed and thoughtful planning, implementation and evaluation of challenging activities across the curriculum can provide opportunities for that development to take place.

## References

BERNHARDT, E. (Ed) (1992) *Life in Language Immersion Classrooms*, Clevedon, Multilingual Matters.

BOURNE, J. (1989) *Moving into the Mainstream*, Windsor, NFER-Nelson.

BOURNE, J. (1994) 'A question of ability', in BOURNE, J. (Ed) *Thinking Through Primary Practice*, London, Routledge.

CUMMINS, J. (1984) 'Implications of bilingual proficiency for the education of minority language students', in ALLEN, P. and SWAIN, M. (Eds) *Language Issues and Education Policies*, ELT Documents 119, The British Council, Oxford, Pergamon Press.

CUMMINS, J. and SWAIN, M. (1986) *Bilingualism in Education*, Longman, New York.

DEPARTMENT FOR EDUCATION (1994) *Draft of National Curriculum Orders for England*, London, SCAA.

ELLIS, G. and BREWSTER, J. (1991) *The Storytelling Handbook for Primary Teachers*, London, Penguin.

LIGHTBOWN, P. and SPADA, N. (1993) *How Languages Are Learned*, Oxford, Oxford University Press.

LUCAS, T., HENZE, R. and DONATO, R. (1990) 'Promoting the success of Latino language-minority students: An exploratory study of six high schools', *Harvard Educational Review*, **60**, 3, pp.315–40.

NORMAN, K. (Ed) (1992) *Thinking Voices: The Work of the National Oracy Project*, London, Hodder and Stoughton.

OFSTED (1994) *Inspection Report 382/2144*, London, HMSO.

OWEN, D. (1994) *Population Trends*, **78**, London, HMSO.

SNOW, C. (1995) 'Change in child language and child linguists', in COLEMAN, H. and CAMERON, L. (Eds) *Change and Language*, Clevedon, Multilingual Matters.

SWAIN, M. and LAPKIN, S. (1982) *Evaluating Bilingual Education: A Canadian Case Study*, Clevedon, Multilingual Matters.

## Resources

BERNHARDT (1992) Detailed studies of American classrooms, illustrating a context very different from the UK.

BOURNE (1989) Gives an overview of mainstream support, its history and development.

ELLIS and BREWSTER (1991) This book takes favourite story books and shows how to exploit the language teaching possibilities. Although aimed at teachers of English as a foreign language in Europe, it may offer insights and ideas for nursery and reception class teachers.

LIGHTBOWN and SPADA (1993) Up to date review of language learning in classroom contexts.

LUCAS, HENZE and DONATO (1990) A report of a study that tried to identify what makes for successful education of minority group pupils, and highlights the importance of making high expectations concrete.

NORMAN (1992) The journal *Talk*, which was published during the National Oracy Project, may also still be available in schools and was a valuable source of ideas.

*Language Materials*

BBC Hindi Urdu Bol chaal

A language course in Hindi/Urdu with video and course book, that could be used in a group or by individuals.

## Language Awareness Resources

CARTER, R. (Ed) (1990) *Knowledge about Language and the Curriculum*, London, Hodder and Stoughton.

A collection of interesting articles on language in education issues; the one by Helen Savva 'The rights of bilingual children' provides a useful complement to this chapter.

### LINC INSET Materials

A collection of materials for use by teachers was produced in 1990 for the 'Language in the National Curriculum' project. Although never published in final form, schools received draft copies which may still be available and some of which are excellent.

HOULTON, D. (1985) *All Our Languages: A Handbook for the Multilingual Classroom*, London, Edward Arnold.
RALEIGH, M. (1980) *The Languages Book*, London, ILEA English Centre.

# Chapter 5

# Learning about the World: Principles and Practice of Global Education

*Margot Brown*

### Principles

> As I looked down, I saw a large river meandering slowly along for miles, passing from one country to another without stopping. I also saw huge forests, extending across several borders. Two words leapt to mind: commonality and interdependence. We are one world. (John-David Bartoe, US Astronaut)

How often do we encourage children to see the world this way? To think of human beings as unified by common needs, and shared aspirations rather than divided by boundaries and differences.

Recognizing and celebrating our uniqueness and our diversity as human beings can also bring us face to face with the elements which bind us together.

> Our lives are inextricably linked by the common thread of humanity.
> If we break it we are all undone. (Oxfam Poster)

Global education is an approach to learning which offers a framework focusing on 'commonality and interdependence'. It highlights areas of the curriculum where a broad world perspective can be included and where the teaching strategies engage the pupils actively in the learning process.

From a very early age children already have formed views about the world around them. These views arise from a variety of influences — family, their own experience, television, story books, advertisements and, of course, school. When Janet Graham and Susan Lynn worked on a research project (1986–8) 'Children's images of "Third World" countries with special reference to pictorial material' they found that many children as young as 6, as well as junior aged children, had strongly stereotyped views of the world. When asked, to sort country name-cards with 'most like' or 'most unlike' Britain, the main discernable criteria used by the children were material living standards and, additionally, by ethnic similarities or differences. Countries in Africa came in the 'most unlike' group due to the children's belief about levels of poverty, prevalent in the press coverage at the time. Other characteristics about the countries were unknown — as indeed were the causes of poverty.

Very little has changed in the nature of press coverage about countries of the South since Graham and Lynn's research. The media still focuses mainly on natural disasters, aid relief (Red Nose Day), and the effects of war. Countries of the world swim in and out of children's consciousness almost totally represented by 'disaster scenarios' — Rwanda, Bangladesh, Zaire. Many others remain anonymous because they have the good fortune not to suffer from major war, earthquake or flood. While it is important for children (and adults) to know and understand the problems encountered by people worldwide, it is also important to learn about them in a broader context. There is a danger that without this context, negative and erroneous stereotypes remain unchallenged. Negative ways of thinking about peoples and places have been found to create barriers to learning in those who hold the negative views (Derman-Sparks, 1989). Schools play a key role in redressing this imbalance.

The National Curriculum has been introduced and implemented since the Lynn and Graham research project was completed. At both Key Stage 1 and Key Stage 2, children are now required to study a 'distant locality'.

Key Stage 1
Two localities should be studied: the locality of the school and a locality, either in the United Kingdom or overseas, in which the physical and/or human features contrast with those in the locality of the school.

Key Stage 2
Three localities should be studied. One study should focus on the locality of the school. . .One locality should be in the United Kingdom and the other in a country in Africa, Asia (excluding Japan), South America or Central America (including the Caribbean). (DfE, 1995)

Sadly, countries studied in geography are not necessarily the focus in history, music or art and so the knowledge of countries may remain flat and one dimensional. Of the statutory orders for Key Stages 1 and 2, those for geography, art and music make most explicit children's entitlement to learn about the wider world of which they are part. There is also no statutory requirement to teach coherently about the diverse nature of communities in the UK — although many teachers still find ways to do so.

### *Why Should Children Learn about the Wider World?*

There are many reasons why learning about the wider world is essential to children's growing understanding of issues, people and places. Students in their second year of teacher training suggested the following reasons when, in a workshop on teaching about distant localities I asked the question 'Why do you think children should learn about life in the wider world?' The list is a compilation of the most frequent suggestions over workshops with nine different groups, training for both Key Stage 1 and Key Stage 2:

- helps to develop appreciation of different cultures;
- helps to understand environmental issues;
- contributes to an understanding of diversity;
- helps develop empathy and respect for different cultures;
- it is a vehicle for other learning;
- through comparison you learn about yourself and your own locality;
- introduces young children to concepts such as 'far away'; and
- gives children an insight into new, different environments and climates and can contribute to understanding different ways of life.

It is also important that in learning about other 'localities', *people* are central. Identifying real people, their families, their hopes and aspirations, their personal past, that of their country and their hoped-for-future, all add a human dimension to 'place'. It is, as the Oxfam poster says, the common thread of humanity which is essential to our understanding of the world. At Key Stage 2 a teaching photo pack such as 'Where camels are better than cars' about life in Mali, West Africa is a good example of this approach.

The wider world is inextricably linked to children's everyday lives. It is not possible to work on a local study, for example, including a visit to the shops, and omit the links to many other countries through the food or the origins of packaging. The 'World in a supermarket bag' simulation activity published by Oxfam is only one of many which can be used to help children explore global links in practical ways. A project on 'Toys and games' also introduces links with countries where the toys are made — from Macau to the United States to Japan. (Japan is unfortunately excluded from Key Stage 2 geography but not from Key Stage 1). Widening children's horizons to recognize how much of local, parochial everyday life is tied to peoples and places far beyond the shores of the United Kingdom is part of understanding how the world works.

Many teachers, working with a new class, find a project about names and naming traditions a valuable way to get to know them. The project can reinforce a sense of self and self-esteem, and support children's sense of identity, and uniqueness. However, it is also true that numerous names in the class, in common with the 'English' language we use, owe their origins to many different national groups. Greek, Celt, Latin, Scandinavian and Hebrew names will be represented in most classes and names with origins in the Indian subcontinent, countries of Africa and the Caribbean will be present in many others. The activity 'Our word house', in the *World Studies 8–13 Handbook* helps children actively explore the cultural diversity of our language roots.

Knowing about 'ourselves' and 'our own culture', so often seen as a priority in schools, also means:

recognising that we live in a multi-ethnic and multi-cultural environment, which has a wonderful diversity of people and places and language and landscapes. The heritage we've evolved over, five, ten, twenty, thirty centuries is inextricably bound up with European, Asiatic and African cultures and the cultures of the 'new world'. These links have been wonderfully enriching, for us and for our children, and will continue to be even more so. We cannot study the UK without recognising the interdependence of our lives with those in other places. (Catling, 1995, p.4)

## Interdependence: A Key Concept in Global Education

Global education is about 'finding out about the world — what's happening now, what has happened in the past, what might come to be in the future' (Steiner, 1993, p.3).

Through learning about communities and localities different from one's own, we come to a keener understanding of our own community. Society in the United Kingdom is varied and diverse. We can use this fact to help us frame questions about the new locality being studied: Questions which concern the roles of women and men, girls and boys; the different faiths, ethnic minority groups, marginalized groups such as travellers or indigenous peoples. We can ask questions about how communities respond to the needs and rights of those with disabilities. To understand a community we also need to know something of its history, its cultural identity through music and art and also about how it is organized, who makes the decisions which affect people living there. We need to understand about how the physical environment affects people and how people have changed their local environment. Ultimately, children can reflect on the rights and responsibilities we all share in respect to the world around us. The following extract from 'Learning from experience' by Miriam Steiner challenges our thinking by reflecting on well-known world inequalities from a different perspective. The relative size of the Swedish and British populations challenges a British audience further by the added dimension of scale.

The world can't afford Sweden
There are 1 000 000 000 Chinese. They have almost certainly many problems but make surprisingly little fuss about them. There are 8 000 000 Swedes. We make an awful fuss about our problems. Think if the reverse was the case, or if there were 1 000 000 000 Swedes, would the world cope with them as well as it copes with 1 000 000 000 Chinese?

We would consume more than 17 000 000 tons of Falun sausage each year, roughly equivalent to a herd of cattle the size of Northern Norway.

Furthermore, should every Swede suddenly decide to take an extra slice of toast for breakfast, we would have to exploit the hydro-electricity produced by six large rivers and build one new nuclear power station.

Would the world support 1 000 000 000 Swedes as it today supports 1 000 000 000 Chinese? I don't know, but we could think about it a while.

Lasse Eriksson, Performer
(Steiner, 1993, p.8)

Reflecting on our impact on the world may encompass fine principles to strive for in educating children for their future lives but how do the disparate strands of learning about another locality, understanding ourselves, considering issues of common human concern and the National Curriculum become interwoven into a manageable unit of work with primary age children? One example comes from a school in inner city Leeds.

## Practice

### *Issues and Process: A Case Study*

Seven Hills is a 'new school'. That is, it is a new building serving the same catchment area as the previous old building, now vacated. In addition, a new housing estate has been built nearby and so numbers are increasing.

In this setting the school is taking on many challenges. Settling in to a new building, tackling the National Curriculum and SATs, LMS, drawing up and implementing policies to develop and sustain the relationships and values which the staff would like to encourage. This is in addition to the myriad daily problems which arise in all schools in inner city locations.

For the headteacher and one particularly enthusiastic member of staff, global education was fundamental to the process of change. They saw global education not only as addressing the issues which are so important for the education of children but also providing the strategies by which these issues could be explored. Global education for this school is a tool of empowerment, integrating values, equal opportunities, active learning skills, self-awareness and behaviour. It is a way of treating children as people and encouraging them to articulate their views on complex issues. Children often are very aware of these issues but require support in expressing their opinions.

One Year 3/Year 4 class, through its termly project, brought together these points to contribute to the schools emerging policy of equal opportunities (including child protection). The project was based on *Journey to Jo'Burg*, by Beverley Naidoo.

### Setting the Scene

The work was originally undertaken as a project on books, part of the English curriculum. It aimed to develop skills of analysis, review, detecting bias, and an understanding of the difference between fact and opinion. The project hoped to demystify the written word and deal with 'real' issues while explaining the concepts of rights and responsibilities and racism as embodied in the apartheid system. The recent changes in South Africa make it possible to use this excellent book for children to compare 'before' and 'after' and to identify the effects of the process of change.

For many children, the written word carries weight and authority but often opinion and fact are confused. In dealing with issues which affect everyday life, the ability to differentiate between fact and opinion is essential. It is a necessary skill in using historical sources and contributes to an understanding of how our view of the world is influenced by our own perspectives.

The aims for the ethos of the classroom included key elements of global education:

- listening skills;
- cooperation;
- rights and responsibilities;
- peaceful conflict resolution;
- the ability to express feelings appropriately; and
- encouragement of equal participation in discussion.

In choosing books for the project it was decided that they should be enjoyable, well-written, exciting, extend reading skills but also raise contemporary issues which would involve the children in honest discussion and debate within a secure environment. The books selected were:

*Journey to Jo'Burg*, Beverley Naidoo;
*Turbulent Term of Tyke Tyler*, Gene Kemp;
*I am David*, Anne Holm;
*Aditi and the One Eyed Monkey*, Suniti Namjoshi.

What did the children do? The project included the following elements:

- what makes a good book;
- learning about South Africa;
- feelings;
- non-violent conflict resolution (including listening skills);
- rights and responsibilities; and
- fact and opinion.

What makes a good book? The children drew up a short list containing their personal choice of what was a good book, and why. For example, 'I think "Window" is a good book because it has good pictures.' They shared their lists in small groups and discussed the reasons for their choices. At this stage, discussion with the teacher began to elicit the definition of opinion and the importance of criteria. For example, one child's 'good pictures' are not necessarily those of another. The discussion on criteria began to highlight story-line, character and description as essential components. To further develop the idea of fact and opinion, the children began to devise questions to ask each other. They decided if the answer was fact or opinion. For example:

- 'It's raining today, isn't it?' — fact/opinion?
- 'I have two sisters?' — fact/opinion?
- 'This is good music, isn't it?' — fact/opinion?

The children also developed their own book reviews around personally chosen books which they had enjoyed.

During work on what makes a good book, the class explored the representation of our diverse and pluralistic society in books. They took a cross section of books from the school library and made a tally of the number of male and female characters in the pictures and also how many were black and how many white. The category most represented was that of white men and boys. This led to a discussion on how we often enjoy books by identifying with the principal characters, how girls feel when the main character is always a boy or black children feel if the main character is always white. It also raised the possibility of story books helping us to understand people who were different from ourselves in some way.

From this introduction of what makes a good book, the children went on to explore what they knew about South Africa.

### Learning about South Africa

#### The Class Brainstorm

They first took part in a class brainstorm. The teacher wrote down all the words or phrases which came into their minds when the words 'South Africa' were spoken.

Some responses from the class:

- starving;
- Ethiopians;
- pretend they're starving to get money from us;
- Santa doesn't go to Africa because they don't look after their toys;
- Nelson Mandela;
- no water/food;
- no houses;
- no cities; and
- very hot.

This response alerted the teacher to the confusion which influenced the children's understanding. The work was then targeted to consider stereotypes and, once again, fact and opinion.

The geographical position of South Africa in relation to the rest of the African Continent was also not at all clear to the children. They were unaware that Africa consists of many countries, many languages, and has many kinds of landscapes. The children were confused about the position of Africa in relation to the rest of the world and this led to some basic map recognition work.

### Journey to Jo'Burg: Getting to Know the Book

Work on the book by Beverley Naidoo now began. The story of 'Journey to Jo'Burg' was read to the children. The class identified strongly with the central characters — a young black South African girl, Naledi and her younger brother Tiro — and their quest to find their mother who had gone to Jo'burg to work. They identified with the excitement of their 'adventure' and their feelings of concern about their sick baby sister, Dineo. Certain scenes made considerable impact on the children and stimulated lively discussion.

One such episode occurs as the two children trek from their grandmother's house to Johannesburg, 300 kilometres away. They have very little food and drink when they set out and when they come across 'rows and rows of orange trees behind barbed wire fences', they climb through the wire to quench their thirst and still their hunger. There they are caught by a young boy who tells them that they will be shot if the farmer catches them. He helps them, however, but through his conversation with the children we learn about punishments meted to black children and adults for offences such as taking a corn-cob when hungry.

When the children finally reach Johannesburg they meet Grace who tells them her story. Her struggle for justice against immense odds made a strong impression on some children in the class and led to work on rights and responsibilities at a later stage of the project.

The different elements of the story stimulated work units on feelings, rights and responsibilities and peaceful conflict resolution in addition to the ongoing work on books. The text was revisited in each of these units linking the concept, the children's own experience and their understanding of the narrative.

### Feelings

Using an illustration from the book, the children wrote what they thought were the feelings of the characters. Thought bubbles were used as part of this activity. They then discussed what other feelings Naledi and Tiro had at different key points in the book and what caused those feelings.

The children worked in small groups to share what circumstances provoked similar feelings in themselves. They discussed which feelings they enjoyed having and which they found difficult to deal with. How did their behaviour change with their feelings? How did they affect other people?

The school was also developing a whole school policy on child protection as part of the Equal Opportunities Policy. The work in the feelings unit complemented this and the children worked through some simple activities on body space and body language.

*Table 5.1: Example of activities on 'feelings'*

A • Brainstorm emotions/feelings which you have.
  • In groups of five or six, use your body to express one of these emotions. Can the others in your group guess which emotion?
  • Take turns.
B • Stand facing a partner, quite a distance apart.
    Move slowly towards one another. Decide at which point you feel uncomfortable about how close you are.
  • Is the distance the same for everyone?
C • Divide the class into two groups.
    One group is told they must try to make and sustain eye contact with members of the other group.
  • The second group is told to avoid eye contact as much as possible.
  • Neither group knows the others' instructions.
  • Both groups circulate for several minutes then change places.
  • Discuss the feelings evoked by both roles and responses.

These activities contributed to a discussion on respecting one another's body space and linked to the rights and responsibilities unit. Poems were constructed using the text at points where feelings played an important part, as when Naledi and Tiro were walking down a long dusty road. The poems used the key words from the text. Thinking about feelings and movement led to work in PE/movement ranging from experimenting with different ways of walking to the following activity which helps develop the skills of judging distance.

*Table 5.2: Activities on 'feelings and movement'*

| | |
|---|---|
| **Aim** | To develop ability to judge distance. |
| **Resources** | One hoop, one beanbag and one blindfold for each pair of children. |
| **Procedures** | One child puts on the blindfold and stands on an agreed spot holding the beanbag. The second child places the hoop at a reasonable distance from the first and then gives directions to the first so that the beanbag can be thrown into the hoop. If the throw is unsuccessful, both discuss how the process could be improved, what language changes are needed to make it easier for the thrower and try again. The pair can then change places and repeat the process. |
| **Comment** | This activity was used in PE but can be used for mathematical language of estimation and measurement, skills of negotiation and listening. |

*Source*: Adapted from an idea in *Cooperative Sports and Games Book* by Terry Orlick.

*Figure 5.1: The two-mules cartoon*

*Source*: Reproduced with permission from Quaker Peace and Service

### Peaceful Conflict Resolution

The units on peaceful conflict resolution and rights and responsibilities had many areas of overlap and strong links to the text. However, in both units the work began with the children's own experiences. The classroom work on conflict resolution linked with the school's work on relationships and behaviour. It also contributed to work on personal and social development.

The unit began with a sequencing activity using the familiar two mules cartoon (Figure 5.1). The picture was cut up into strips and each group of children put them into a sequence they felt told the story. They then developed dialogues for the pictures, giving names to the animals and writing the dialogue as a play. They also wrote contexts for the situation as it appeared in the cartoon; for example the farmer had shouted at one mule who became grumpy and wouldn't talk to the other. Throughout, emphasis had been laid on the role of listening and language, exploring how difficult it can be to retrace steps, once something has been said in anger.

The children then acted out their dialogues, reflecting again about fact and opinion. Finally they suggested conflicts which occurred in their experience. Issues of conflict which the children raised included:

- who had the best toys;
- who was getting up at night to feed the baby;
- paying bills; and
- problems caused by drinking.

The children developed role-play around the situation in which they were involved and considered the role of language in defusing or escalating a situation. They agreed that when you are angry you don't listen well and this can stop you finding a solution. The role of listener came under scrutiny. What constitutes a good listener? Some of the qualities of a good listener which the children agreed on were:

- look at the speaker in the eye;
- make 'mm' noises;
- sit still, don't fidget;
- don't interrupt;
- don't walk away;
- ask questions; and
- try to be interested.

The children put their work on listening into an assembly on good listening, using role-play.

*Assembly*

The theme of the assembly was 'You have a choice: With careful listening and good communication we can sort things out without being violent.' The children acted out:

- listening skill activities;
- giving positive feedback;
- two mules dialogue; and
- a real life situation peacefully resolved.

### Rights and Responsibilities

This was the next unit of the project. The class already had 'rules' — only five:

1  We will try to be fair and not use differences as insults.
2  We will listen to each other.
3  We will have fun.
4  We will do nothing to put others in danger.
5  We will not fight.

These 'rules' had been set at the beginning of the school year and the class now reflected back to that time and discussed:

- Why do we have rules?
- Are they a good idea?

The outcome of the discussion included dropping the term 'rules' and replacing it with 'rights'. Further discussion led to the idea of responsibilities. There are suggestions for appropriate resources at the end of this chapter on rights and responsibilities. This work led to useful discussion on 'what is bullying?' The most popular right at the end of this work was 'Everyone has a right to make a mistake.'

Rights issues raised by 'Journey to Jo'Burg' were also discussed. Who has the power to refuse people's rights? Why do they do so? What can people do? Can change happen? What do we know about places where people's rights are not respected? Specific issues such as: where to live; catching a particular bus; medical issues; and pass laws; were discussed in the light of changes which have taken place in South Africa.

The children knew that the Pass Laws and segregation on buses no longer apply, though not many white people travel by bus. The Groups Areas Act has been dropped although *de facto* segregation largely continues. The children discussed how easy or difficult it is to change how people think, particularly if opinions have been held for a long time but also how important it is for change to take place.

To learn about the changes and to support work on fact and opinion, the children wrote letters to various organizations who offer information on South Africa:

- South African Embassy;
- South African Tourist Board;
- Oxfam;
- UNICEF;
- ANC;
- Anti-Apartheid; and
- British Defence and Aid Fund for Southern Africa.

The pictorial materials sent by some of the above were also scrutinized for balance, as had been the school library at the beginning of the project. Some tourist material showed no black South Africans at all. This point was noted by the children and related to issues raised by the book and to the recent changes. This contributed to their discussion on change.[1]

## Conclusion

Understanding the concept of change at a variety of levels from personal to global is not an easy task for primary age children but exploring it through active learning and literature can support that process.

Through the case-study outlined here, the children engaged in practical work in English, and PSE; through their developing understanding of 'change' and 'fact/opinion' they were working with historical skills in addition to understanding 'place' in geography.

The topic used 'Journey to Jo'Burg' to stimulate thinking about issues of common human concern in children's own lives and that of children in distant localities, breaking down the barriers and boundaries which do so little to contribute to a fair and just world.

## Note

1   We wish to thank Jane McMahon and her class and Kathy Thompson, headteacher Seven Hills School, Leeds.

## References

CATLING, S. (1995) *Wider Horizons: The Children's Charter*, Primary Geography.

DERMAN-SPARKS, L. (1989) *Anti-bias Curriculum, Tools for Empowering Young Children*, Washington, DC, National Association for the Education of Young Children.

DfE (1995) *Geography in the National Curriculum* London, HMSO.

FISHER, S. and HICKS, D. (1985) 'Word house activity,' in *World Studies 8–13 Handbook*, Harlow, Oliver and Boyd.

GRAHAM, J. and LYNN, S. (1988) *Children's Images of 'Third World' Countries with Special Reference to Pictorial Material*, London, South Bank Polytechnic.

HOLM, A. (1986) *I am David*, London, Magnet.

KEMP, G. (1977) *The Turbulent Term of Tyke Tyler*, London, Puffin.

NAIDOO, B. (1991) *Journey to Jo'Burg*, London, Young Lions.

NAMJOSHI, S. (1986) *Aditi and the One-eyed Monkey*, London, Sheba Feminist Publishers.

ORLICK, T. (1978) *Cooperative Sports and Games Book*, London, Writers and Readers Publishing Cooperative.

STEINER, M. (1993) *Learning from Experience, World Studies in the Primary Curriculum*, Stoke-on-Trent, Trentham Books.

### Resources

- BROWN, M. (Ed) (1995) *Our World, Our Rights: Teaching about Rights and Responsibilities in the Primary School* a handbook for learning about the Universal Declaration of Human Rights London, Amnesty International.
- BUTLER, J. *Art Against Apartheid*, London, Art and Development Education 5–16 Project Oxfam Education.
- ORLICK, T. (1982) *The Second Cooperative Sports and Games Book*, New York, Pantheon Books (Random House).
- *Teachers Handbook, The Whole Child, It's Our Right, Keep Us Safe* (1993) Four guides for teachers on introducing the UN Convention on the Rights of the Child across the curriculum, London, UK, Save The Children and UNICEF.
- *Where Camels are Better than Cars.* A locality study in Mali, West Africa for Key Stage 2 from Development Education Centre, Gillett Centre, 998 Bristol Road, Selly Oak, Birmingham B29 6LE.
- *World in a Supermarket Bag.* An activity on food for 7–11-year-olds from Oxfam, 274 Banbury Rd, Oxford OX2 7DZ.
- Schools can contact Letterbox Library, Unit 2D, Leroy House, 436 Essex Road, London N1 3QP for non-sexist books and books for a multicultural society.

# Chapter 6

# Teaching, Learning and the Environment

*Joy Palmer*

## Background

In the minds of some primary educationists, the words 'environmental education' no doubt conjure up ideas of a crucial cross-curricular theme; an essential
aspect of the curriculum entitlement of every young child growing up to be a
mature citizen of tomorrow's world, an exciting and motivating area of study
with direct relevance for the quality of life in the twenty-first century. For
others, the words will no doubt have mental associations with such phrases as
'not a statutory requirement', 'peripheral to the defined core', 'not enough
time', and 'hardly a priority in an over-burdened curriculum'. Both views represent reality. My every sympathy extends to busy primary classroom teachers
and students of education who recognize the importance of teaching and
learning relating to the environment, yet do constant battle with the serious
time constraints of classrooms and curriculum plans. There are no easy answers to such tensions; no magical formula for incorporating a crucial cross-
curricular theme into primary schooling without spending time and paying
careful attention to its content and delivery. It is the purpose of this chapter
to assist with that incorporation; to provide succinct guidelines and advice on
planning for the successful inclusion of environmental education in the primary school curriculum, and to demonstrate how the statutory curriculum
actually goes a long way towards providing a ready framework for the coverage of many essential aspects of the theme. In addition to such practical help,
the chapter aims to provide an up-to-date view of what school-based environmental education actually entails, and to highlight its ever-increasing global
importance. In short, the following pages bring together a combination of
some of the theoretical and practical aspects of teaching and learning in this
curriculum area, and support a justification for the recognition of its fundamental importance in the formal education of all young people. Environmental
education should not be left to chance.

*Joy Palmer*

## Environmental Education: Definitions and Development

The Education Reform Act of 1988 and the associated introduction of the National Curriculum for schools in England and Wales heralded the firm placement of environmental education on the curriculum map of schools; a move that was greatly welcomed by those working in, and promoting, this field of study. This was accomplished by the establishment of cross-curricular elements of the whole curriculum which were intended to permeate and augment the statutory core and foundation subjects. Cross-curricular elements were deemed by the National Curriculum Council and the Curriculum Council for Wales to include:

- **skills**: communication, numeracy, study, problem-solving, personal and social and information technology;
- **dimensions**: equal opportunities and preparation for life in a multicultural society;
- **themes**: environmental education, economic and industrial understanding, citizenship, health education and careers education and guidance.

These elements are outlined in *Curriculum Guidance 3: The Whole Curriculum* (NCC, 1990a) and *The Whole Curriculum 5–16 in Wales* (CCW, 1991). As a whole, they are intended to:

promote discussion of values and beliefs, extend knowledge and understanding, encourage practical activities and decision-making and further the inter-relationship of the individual and the community. (NCC, 1990a, p.3)

Thus environmental education was defined as one of the named cross-curricular themes of the National Curriculum and, as such, had an agreed definition and content as discussed in the National Curriculum Council's document devoted entirely to this theme: *Curriculum Guidance 7: Environmental Education* (NCC, 1990b). These published guidelines outline the core aims of environmental education as follows:

- to provide opportunities to acquire the knowledge, values and attitudes, commitment and skills needed to protect and improve the environment;
- to encourage pupils to examine and interpret the environment from a variety of perspectives — physical, geographical, biological, sociological, economic, political, technological, historical, aesthetic, ethical and spiritual; and
- to arouse pupils' awareness and curiosity about the environment and encourage active participation in resolving environmental problems. (NCC, 1990b, p.3)

The national guidelines also provide an overview of objectives to be covered in the design and implementation of programmes of work in environmental education. These include objectives expressed in terms of attitudes to be promoted, such as appreciation of care and concern for the environment, independent thought, respect for the beliefs and opinions of others, respect for evidence and argument, tolerance and open-mindedness. Other objectives are expressed in terms of cross-curricular skills: communication, numeracy, study, problem-solving, personal and social, and information technology skills. A third and final set of objectives relates to areas of knowledge and understanding to be pursued through this cross-curricular theme; including knowledge and understanding of natural processes, of human impact on the environment, environmental issues of importance in the world today, change over time, legislation and decision-making, conflicts, interdependence, actions and consequences of actions, design, aesthetics, and protection and management.

More will be said of these objectives a little later. At this stage, suffice to say that *Curriculum Guidance 7* promotes the fundamental idea that environmental education is an essential part of every pupil's curriculum; not as an isolated and discrete unit of study, but as something that informs and permeates teaching and learning of the separate core and foundation subjects whilst embodying elements of its own 'subject matter knowledge'. Without doubt, environmental education as portrayed at the time of the introduction of the National Curriculum for Schools was to be interpreted as far more than a single school subject consisting of knowledge to be gained and facts to be learned. Rather, 'It helps to encourage awareness of the environment, leading to informed concern for and active participation in resolving environmental problems. . . .It aims to develop in young people the skills, knowledge, understanding and values which will enable them to make informed decisions and take action for the environment' (NCC, 1990b, Foreword).

The present day scene, only a few years after the publication of *Curriculum Guidance 7*, looks very different — at least as far as published documentation is concerned. Significant revisions of the National Curriculum content, in operation from September 1995, effectively redefined the curriculum's statutory elements and left serious doubts in the minds of many as to whether previously documented (and not revised) cross-curricular themes have any formally acknowledged place in the curriculum at all. Alongside the apparent 'disappearance' of themes in these revisions, the content of key subject areas that clearly include and inter-relate with elements of the subject-matter of environmental education (notably science and geography) was substantially altered. Major questions of this new era of Statutory Orders must therefore include: are we, as educators of students, teachers and pupils, back to 're-inventing the wheel' as far as the content and objectives of environmental education are concerned? Along similar lines, have we regressed in terms of our understanding of how 'curriculum space' may be organized to include environmental education as an effective cross-curricular element? My short answer to both of these key questions is 'no'. Environmental education is well on the map of the revised curriculum, and recent changes actually increase flexibility for teachers to plan appropriate programmes of work. This theme will of course be returned to, but first it is appropriate to broaden this over-view and discussion of developments to a level well beyond the 'local' scene. Policy and practice in the UK must be viewed in the context of a complex backcloth of global landmarks and initiatives that have contributed to both national and international understanding of what effective environmental edu-cation is, and perhaps ought to be, in the schools of the world today.

With limited space available, this chapter can only contain an at-a-glance guide to significant events and documents that have influenced international thinking and action in this field. For those readers wishing to pursue a history of international developments in greater depth, attention is drawn to such overviews as those provided by Sterling (1992) and Palmer and Neal (1994). Table 6.1 provides a summary of key dates and events in a timeline of inter-national developments.

It can be seen from Table 6.1 that environmental education has become widely recognized for its significance over a period of around twenty-five years. Urgent pleas have been made at a number of substantial gatherings and in widely acclaimed documents for the translation of global definitions, objec-tives and principles into policies, programmes and resources at national and community levels.

It should be noted that alongside this upsurge of interest in environmental education, numerous other related 'adjectival educations' have found their ways on to the stage: development education, global education, peace educa-tion, citizenship education and human rights education all have their place in the global agenda for the promotion of pro-environmental behaviours and the improvement of the quality of human life. The development and existence of these various inter-linked approaches to environmentalism are an indication of the tremendous energy that has been and is currently being devoted to the promotion of planned processes which enable participants to explore and understand the environment and to take action to make the world a better place for all forms of life.

## Towards a Sustainable Future: Core Concepts and Curriculum Content

Global acknowledgment of the centrality and importance of the concept of sustainable development in environmental education is the hallmark of the 1990s. Developments in the philosophy, policies and practice of the field through time leading to that position have been myriad and complex. In most generalized terms, they have transformed the dominant view of environmental education from one of teaching about nature, with 'show-and-tell' techniques of the early 1970s; to one of teaching through experiential fieldwork and values education in the 1980s; to one of action research, and pupil-led

Table 6.1:   Timeline of key dates in the global history of environmental education

| | | | |
|---|---|---|---|
| Alleged first use of term 'environmental education' at IUCN meeting, Paris | 1948 | | |
| | | 1968 | UNESCO Biosphere conference Paris acknowledges importance of environmental education |
| IUCN/UNESCO meeting, Nevada, USA. Formulation of a key definition* widely adopted around the world | 1970 | | |
| | | 1972 | UN Conference on the 'Human Environment', Stockholm, Sweden |
| UNESCO/UNEP International Workshop on Environmental Education, Belgrade, Yugoslavia. Founding of International Environmental Education Programme. The Belgrade Charter, which produced a set of guiding principles for EE | 1975 | | |
| | | 1977 | UNESCO Intergovernmental Conference on EE, Tbilisi, USSR, established a framework for international concensus on EE |
| | | 1980 | The World Conservation Strategy launched, and promoted the key concept of 'sustainable development' |
| UNESCO/UNEP International Congress on Environmental Education and Training, Moscow, Russia. WCED Report: *Our Common Future*, concerned with environment and development issues | 1987 | | |
| | | 1988 | European Community resolution on EE identified EE as an entitlement for every school pupil in the Community |
| IUCN launch of *Caring for the Earth: A strategy for Sustainable Living*, which set out nine principles of sustainable living, and stressed the central role of education in achieving these | 1991 | | |
| | | 1992 | UN Conference on 'Environment and Development': 'The Earth Summit: Rio-de-Janeiro, Brazil. Launch of *Agenda 21* Strengthening of European Resolution on EE |

*Note*: * Environmental education is the process of recognizing values and clarifying concepts in order to develop skills and attitudes necessary to understand and appreciate the inter-relatedness among man, his culture and his biophysical surroundings (IUCN, 1970).

problem-solving fieldwork in the 1990s. Commonly used terms of the present day are 'empowerment' and 'capacity building', concepts that embrace the critical importance of personal involvement, action and decision-making. Core issues underpinning environmental education of today are equality, social justice, inter-species justice and inter-generational justice. In other words, environmental education has progressed to a state of incorporating a vision of environmental issues that is far wider than a study of ecology and environmental science; it is a vision which encompasses all aspects of sustainable living within life-support systems and processes.

If environmental education programmes are to address the complexities of such matters as sustainable development, and issues of quality of life, equality and justice, then a defined core content of knowledge and understanding about the environment will be necessary. Learners will need a context in which to develop conceptual understanding.

Various attempts have been made at an international level to arrive at a consensus of a core content of knowledge for environmental education programmes, but at this point in the chapter it is perhaps appropriate to return to the established curriculum in the UK. Curriculum Guidance 7 defines *knowledge* objectives for the theme as follows:

As a basis for making informed judgements about the environment pupils should develop knowledge and understanding of:

- the natural processes which take place in the environment;
- the impact of human activities on the environment;
- different environments, both past and present;
- environmental issues such as the greenhouse effect, acid rain, air pollution;
- local, national and international legislative controls to protect and manage the environment; how policies and decisions are made about the environment;
- the environmental interdependence of individuals, groups, communities and nations;
- how human lives and livelihoods are dependent on the environment;
- the conflicts which can arise about environmental issues;
- how the environment has been affected by past decisions and actions;
- the importance of planning, design and aesthetic considerations; and
- the importance of effective action to protect and manage the environment.

(NCC, 1990b, p.4)

The same document suggests that a basic knowledge and understanding of the environment can be developed through the following topics:

- climate;
- soils, rocks and minerals;
- water;
- materials and resources, including energy;
- plants and animals;
- people and their communities;
- buildings, industrialisation and waste.

(ibid., p.7)

It was envisaged at the outset of National Curriculum implementation that generally these topics will be taught through core and foundation subjects, and in particular through the attainment targets and programmes of study for science, technology, geography and history. The *revised* statutory orders contain a substantial framework for teaching essential aspects of knowledge and understanding of environmental education. Environmental content is particularly well represented in geography and in science; there are important references to it in technology and opportunities in other subjects. Pupils are required, progressively, to consider the concept of sustainable development and make value judgments about sustainable behaviour and related conflicts of interest. A summary of some of the key locations of environmental education within the revised orders for geography and science for Key Stages 1 and 2 is provided at the end of this chapter in Appendix A, though readers are encouraged to study the entire documentation themselves as there is much relevance to environmental education elsewhere.

As previously mentioned, the presently specified curriculum allows teachers considerable flexibility in planning appropriate schemes of work and learning tasks which address identified knowledge objectives.

### Beyond a Knowledge Base

So far this chapter has placed emphasis on *content* of environmental education, i.e., on subject knowledge, understanding and core concepts. Yet inextricably interwoven with this are the other two dimensions of the learning process: skills and attitudes. Again, these are referred to and discussed in a variety of documents which attempt to define the aims and content of environmental education. For example:

### Knowledge and Skills

I   To develop a coherent body of knowledge about the environment, both built and rural, sufficient to recognise actual and potential problems,

II  To be able to gather information from or about the environment independently or as part of a co-operative activity,

III   To be able to consider different opinions related to environmental issues and to arrive at a balanced judgement,

IV   To appreciate the ways in which environmental issues are interrelated so that one factor affects others,

V   To be able to evaluate information about the environment from different sources and to try to resolve environmental problems,

VI   To understand and to know how to use the mechanisms available in society for bringing about environmental change.

### Attitudes and Behaviour

I   To develop an appreciation of the environment and critical awareness of the natural and built environment,

II   To develop an attitude of concern for environmental matters and a wish to improve environmental understanding,

III   To be critical of one's own environmental attitudes and to take steps to change one's own behaviour and actions,

IV   To have a desire to participate in initiatives to care for or improve the environment,

V   To wish to participate in environmental decision-making and to make opinions known publicly.

(CEE, 1987, p.6)

### Skills

- communication skills;
- numeracy skills;
- study skills;
- problem-solving skills;
- personal and social skills; and
- information technology skills.

### Attitudes

Promoting positive attitudes to the environment is essential if pupils are to value it and understand their role in safeguarding it for the future. Encouraging the development of the attitudes and personal qualities below will contribute to this process:

- appreciation of, and care and concern for the environment and for other living things;
- independence of thought on environmental issues;
- a respect for the beliefs and the opinions of others;
- a respect for evidence and rational argument; and
- tolerance and open-mindedness.

(NCC, 1990b, p.6)

Environmental education in practice is thus far more than 'knowledge to be gained and facts to be learned'. The National Curriculum clearly regards it as an essential part of every pupil's curriculum, with three-fold interconnecting aims, as published and detailed earlier in this chapter. We have seen that these aims involve the provision of opportunities (to acquire knowledge, values, attitudes, commitment and skills); the examination and interpretation of the environment from a variety of perspectives; the arousal of awareness and curiosity about the environment; and the encouragement of active participation in resolving environmental problems.

The key to successful implementation and achievement of the worthy yet rather theoretically sounding aims and objectives so far outlined undoubtedly rests on the skills of *planning*, at all levels. No teacher or school can leave environmental education to chance; as an essential part of every pupil's curriculum, it must be planned for with as much care and attention to detail as any other aspect of teaching and learning.

Theoretical principles pertaining to the theme need thoughtful interpretation into practice. All pupils should have experiences of problem solving, decision making and participation in relation to the environment. Attendant considerations should include ecological, political, economic, social, aesthetic, technological and ethical aspects. A teacher's task is about helping individuals to consider their own actions; empowering them to choose behaviours that will help to solve existing environmental problems and avoid the creation of new ones. So let us now turn attention to what this rather complex guidance may actually mean in practice.

## Planning for Inclusion of Environmental Education in the Primary Curriculum

Planning for the inclusion of environmental education in the curriculum needs to take account of three interlinked components which I will term the 'structural elements' of the theme:

- education about the environment (that is, basic knowledge and understanding of the environment);
- education for the environment (concerned with values, attitudes and positive action for the environment); and
- education in or through the environment (that is, using the environment as a resource with emphasis on enquiry and investigation).

The 'dimensions' of skills, concepts and attitudes are inextricably bound into the core content of these elements:

- Education *about* the environment has the purpose of developing knowledge and understanding about values and attitudes.

- Education *for* the environment encourages pupils to explore their personal response to and relationship with the environment and environmental issues. This is linked to the development of attitudes and values, including elements of human understanding and behaviour necessary for the development of sustainable and caring use of the environment.
- Education *in* or *through* the environment uses the environment as a resource for learning. It is a resource which enables the development of considerable knowledge and understanding as well as skills of investigation and communication.

The structural elements, like the dimensions of learning, are of course, inter-related and are essential components of planning at every level, ranging from whole-school and year-group curriculum planning to the more specific planning of topics and tasks applicable to a class, group of learners or an individual pupil. A key part of the planning process must take account of the need to develop an understanding of the inter-relationship between the theme's various components. This is likely to be achieved through elaboration of content of environmental education (perhaps the seven 'topics' or areas of knowledge and understanding listed above), and the development of related skills, concepts and attitudes.

Figure 6.1 represents the components of environmental education in diagrammatic form. The dimensions of skills, concepts and attitudes are inextricably bound into the core content of the three structural elements. Teachers could well use this model as a checklist of the components to be borne in mind when undertaking curriculum planning. It expands upon the three-fold framework which underpins planning: tasks should be planned that educate about the environment, for the environment, and that involve practical activities in the environment. Within this framework are located three crucial elements expressed from the point of view of the individual, i.e., personal experience in the environment, the development of personal concern for the environment, and the taking of personal action in, and on behalf of, the environment. Curriculum plans need to take account of the inclusion of all of these elements, by providing appropriate learning tasks and experiences. Using this model as a framework, teachers can then elaborate upon the details, perhaps in table, list, or flow chart forms. Precise learning objectives can be 'spelled out', in relation to learning for, and about, the environment in any specific topic or subject-based plan of work. These can then be linked to the Programmes of Study, Attainment Targets and levels of the core and foundation subjects. Furthermore, they can be linked to planned experiences and investigatory work in the environment; and attitudes that it is planned to promote with the aim of encouraging the development of environmental concern and action.

The model provided in Figure 6.2 can be used as the basis for planning a single topic or series of lessons; and most importantly, for linking environmental

Figure 6.1:   *Model of teaching and learning in environmental education*

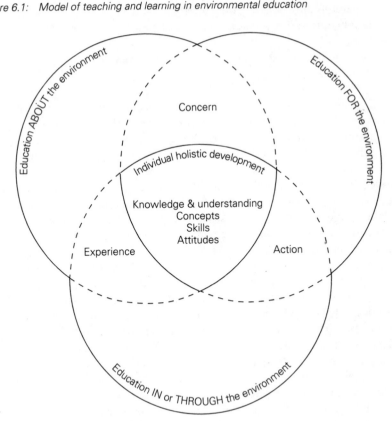

*Source*:  J.A. Palmer (1994) and first published in Palmer, J.A. and Neal, P.D. (1994)

education work within a topic or lessons into a coherent and progressive overall curriculum plan.

### Principles into Practice

There can be no single 'right or wrong' way to approach the inclusion of environmental education in the primary school curriculum. When the theme was originally included in the National Curriculum, guidelines suggested that a variety of approaches is best, and that five possible timetabling arrangements can be identified which cater for the inclusion of cross-curricular themes in the curriculum. These are:

1   taught through National Curriculum and other subjects;
2   whole curriculum planning leading to blocks of activities (e.g., a series of subject-based topics lasting for varying periods of time);

3  separately timetabled cross-curricular themes;
4  taught through separately timetabled personal and social educa-
    tion; and
5  long-block timetabling (e.g., an activity week).
(NCC, 1990b, p.15)

It is most probable that in the primary school, the first two of these
approaches will be the ones most commonly adopted. Environmental starting
points and tasks — ranging from pond-dipping or observing traffic in a con-
gested urban high street to constructing a compost heap or noting the effects
of pollution in a stream — can successfully be developed into formal teaching
grounded in the content of the National Curriculum for science or geography;
or they can be the unifying element in integrated topic work which again
addresses content of the core and foundation subjects. In the reality of major
time constraints facing schools, environmental education is no doubt best
included in the curriculum by using a combination of these two approaches
and perhaps also by pursuing shorter topics which address specific environmental concepts, issues or experiences in non-directed time. Whichever approach or combination of approaches is utilized, it is essential that first-hand
experiences of the environment — call these fieldwork if you so wish — are
at the forefront of teaching and learning. Furthermore, such field engagement
need not be costly either in terms of time or money. The most important
resource available to every teacher and school is the immediate locality (whether
this be rural or urban) and of course, the school grounds themselves. By
introducing pupils to the investigation and management of a small area such
as the school grounds, they will be helped to develop a sense of responsibility
and to realize that places (including those at a local level) can be managed in
ways that encourage sustainability. The teacher's task then is to help learners
appreciate how principles applied on a small scale can be relevant to much
larger scale habitats and issues.

There is an almost limitless choice of themes to pursue in the local area.
Extensive resources are available on such topics as weather, homes, traffic,
shopping, wildlife, energy, ponds, trees, litter, water, food and farming, buildings, etc., which can incorporate out-of-classroom investigations in almost any
location. Beyond such 'well tried and tested' themes, more challenging issue-
based topics and studies relating in some instances to distant environments
and global issues will encourage understanding of the key concepts underpinning environment and development issues. Again, the choice of such themes
is almost limitless. Common topics for which extensive published material is
available include pollution, oceans, Antarctica, tropical rain forests, acid rain,
waste materials, population increase, the greenhouse effect, food production
and endangered species. Figure 6.2 provides an outline topic web developed
and used by a Key Stage 2 teacher on the theme of trees. This lists a range of
activities undertaken by the pupils in a variety of settings including the classroom, playground and local woodland. It shows how such activities were

*Figure 6.2: Trees: Suggested activities and cross-curricular links*

**Geography**

- Discover location of World's rain forests
- Investigate importance of forests
- Draw diagrams to show forest layers and add appropriate birds, animals, insects
- Investigate the impact of deforestation on the environment and forms of life
- Discuss how people around the world can show concern for preserving rain forests (as nations and as individuals)
- Set up a paper recycling scheme
- Investigate schemes in the community

**Mathematics**

- Measure height and girth of local trees
- Research heights of typical rain forest trees to compare
- Map a woodland area
- Classify trees into sets
- Research rates of rain forest loss around the world

**Science**

- Consider what a tree is
- Closely obreve trees
- Draw trees and label parts
- Investigate a tree's basic needs
- Grow a tree: find out about factors affecting germination and growth
- Identify trees. Discuss classification and use of keys
- Do experiments on chlorophyll loss and photosynthesis
- Investigate woodland life
- Construct food chains and webs
- Investigate decomposition

**Art**

- Do painting/printing/needlecraft of trees, forests, chlorophyll loss
- Make model of rain forest village
- Construct a frieze to show forest layers and life
- Design rain forest conservation posters

**Trees and Forests**

**English**

- Make a 'tree dictionary' including all relevant vocabulary
- Write factual accounts about trees, forests and the impact of tree removal
- Do creative writing on similar themes
- Read stories and poems about rain forest life

**Music**

- Make sounds depicting life in a rain forest. Compose a 'rain forest symphony'
- Listen to published music on the theme of trees and forests

**Religious Education**

- Read Bible stories associated with trees
- Pursue the idea of personal concern and responsibility for the World

*Note:* Issues to be addressed throughout topic: Management of resources, conservation, deforestation, endangered species, degradation, habitat destruction, effect of climate on life

linked to the teaching of the core and foundation subjects of the curriculum whilst comprising an environmental topic in their own right. This is also an excellent example of how a teacher may go beyond a 'local', common topic, i.e., trees, to challenge pupils to investigate and develop awareness of global issues and key concepts related to them. Furthermore, the topic web suggests that the children were actively involved in investigation and problem-solving tasks relating to the theme.

It could well be argued that whether environmental education be an infusion of environment and development issues into all disciplines (i.e., truly cross-curricular), or whether it is treated as a subject or an aspect of other subjects, is actually irrelevant. Inevitably these options complement and over-lap with each other; together they provide flexibility for a curriculum which has relevance for young lives and which is characterized by active learning processes.

If all of this rather academic-sounding guidance is ever to be successful in practice, then clearly there are whole school matters to be addressed. En-vironmental education, like every other subject, needs leadership, coordina-tion, a whole school policy, assessment with record-keeping arrangements, and resources. Quite clearly, a single chapter cannot do justice to a discussion of these matters, and the attention of readers wishing to pursue whole school matters in greater depth is drawn to *The Handbook of Environmental Educa-tion* (Palmer and Neal, 1994). Leadership and coordination are essential, and it is possible to achieve this through variations on the following basic patterns:

- an individual coordinator and curriculum leader for environmental education;
- an individual responsible for all cross-curricular themes;
- a committee or team for coordinating environmental education (per-haps with representatives of each key stage of year group);
- a committee or team for coordinating all cross-curricular themes; and
- an understanding that every individual teacher has the task of incor-porating environmental education in the curriculum of his or her own class.

Whilst the last arrangement may seem haphazard, it can work well in a small school situation with cooperative and committed staff. Ideally, there would be an individual in a position to coordinate the theme throughout a school, backed up by an organized, formal system of communication, plan-ning and monitoring. A prime task of the coordinator must be to facilitate the implementation of the school's policy for environmental education, or to es-tablish such policy and guidelines for its implementation if these do not exist. Help and advice for this task will be found in the sources listed in the biblio-graphy below. I suggest that a policy document may be organized under ten headings:

- aims;
- objectives;
- methods of teaching (rooted in direct experience);
- timetabling arrangements;
- components (knowledge, understanding, skills, concepts, attitudes);
- scope (local to regional to global);
- resources and organization of resources;
- assessment, record-keeping, evaluation;
- the 'school' and its grounds as a resource; and
- school involvement in community action.

In many ways, the final two headings above underpin all others. No school will be successful in its endeavours without discussion and taking account of all areas of school life which contribute to teaching and learning about the environment. These include not only the formal curriculum, but also extra-curricular activities such as school clubs, membership of national societies, etc.; the whole school ethos, meaning its community spirit and its overall promotion of positive attitudes towards the environment; special events, such as environmental days/weeks/festivals and competitions; and school involvement with parents and the community, including taking part in local projects and monitoring local issues.

A useful way of assessing the contribution of all areas of school life to the promotion of environmental knowledge and concern is by the use of an 'environmental audit'. From the results of this, ideas for inclusion in policy and curriculum documents may well emerge. The content of such an audit will be designed to suit the needs of the particular institution. Emphasis will depend on whether the school already has a policy or whether the audit is being used as a way into establishing such a document. Baczala (1992) suggests ten main questions which an environmental audit may address:

1   How is the school as an institution encouraging environmental education?
2   How is environmental education managed?
3   Is the school developing appropriate and useful documentation relating to environmental education?
4   What evidence is there that environmental education is being integrated into the curriculum?
5   How do pupils perceive the relevance of environmental education in their learning?
6   What arrangements does the school have for fieldwork?
7   What are the arrangements for assessment in environmental education? Is achievement acknowledged?
8   Is there evidence that the school estate is used as a learning resource?
9   What are the arrangements for co-ordinating the management of the school estate?

10   To what extent does the school manage itself with respect for the
     environment (practise what it preaches)?
(Baczala, 1992)

A well-planned and executed audit will have many advantages aside from
contributing to a policy document; it will strengthen environmental awareness
within the school at all levels (pupils, teachers, parents, governors); it will help
safeguard the environment and improve its quality; it will identify potential
cost, energy and waste-saving mechanisms; it will facilitate interchange of
information and cooperation between teachers and should lead to more successful integration of environmental teaching across the curriculum.

No school need be short of resource material for environmental education. One of the key tasks of the coordinator must be to make an assessment
of, and document, the potential of the school's own locality as a resource, and
to systematize the collection and organization of other key resources.[1] The
following guidelines may be helpful:

- Keep a record book on the local area, with details of its potential as
  a resource. You may include in this brochures about stately homes,
  museums, etc., open to the public, times when your local parish church
  staff may welcome school parties, local sites of historic or other environmental interest, transport routes, farms which welcome school visits, maps, aerial and other photographs, lists of interesting buildings,
  industries, shops, etc.
- Make regular contact with the local library; be aware of its collections of
  materials on both the local area and on environmental issues in general.
- Build up an environmental section in your own school library and
  resource area with books, pictures, wall charts, videos, audio-
  cassettes, computer programmes, slides, etc.
- Keep up-to-date with the many TV and radio programmes broadcast
  on environmental issues; make recordings within the restrictions of
  copyright.
- Organize the collection and display of regular incoming items from
  such associations as the RSPB, WWF and Tidy Britain Group; consider
  joining these and becoming a member of the National Association for
  Environmental Education.
- Monitor the news. A valuable resources bank can be established by
  collecting news cuttings relating to environmental issues. If a major
  event occurs, e.g., oil spillage or nuclear accident, media coverage
  could be collected into a substantial case study.

**Conclusion**

It is now generally accepted that children come to understand and to develop
personal behaviours in the world through active learning in a wide range of
social situations. In the context of this chapter, active learning about, for, and

in the environment involves a judicious mix of 'teaching' or 'telling' and of direct experiences. It involves the use of appropriate resources and tools for investigating and considering issues — and most importantly, it requires opportunities to develop the capacities to act on ideas generated. Sound programmes of environmental education, whether they be topic or subject-based will help young learners gain a deep appreciation of the world of nature. They will also go significantly beyond this to demonstrate that the environment is not just plants, animals and the physical world: it is also people and social structures. Associated with complex patterns of social, political and economic activity within the biological and physical world are critical issues that require urgent attention at a global level.

Effective environmental education will enable every individual to understand and recognize factors that influence both the nature and the quality of the environment (both local and global). It will empower individuals to develop the capacities to engage in informed debate about environmental matters and to adopt pro-environmental behaviours.

The primary school years are clearly the critical period in which individuals should begin the lifetime long environmental education process. Research in progress (Palmer, 1993a) shows that childhood experience in the natural environment is the single most significant influence affecting development of concern for the environment in later years; surely a powerful reinforcement of the importance of educating *in* the environment. The same research study (Palmer, 1993b) provides evidence which demonstrates that many young children coming into formal schooling at the age of 4 have already acquired a wide knowledge repertoire relating both to their local environment and to wider issues. Effective teaching will develop this base of existing knowledge and understanding; eliminate misconceptions brought to the learning situation, and counteract biased and stereotypical ideas about the world and its people that may be held by the pupils. This task cannot be left to chance. Successful teaching depends upon planned processes and experiences, and the recognition that environmental education can have a central rather than a peripheral place in a broad, balanced curriculum.

# Appendix A

## The Place of Environmental Education in the Geography Curriculum

### Key Stage 1 Programme of Study

1 Pupils should be given opportunities to:

a investigate the physical and human features of their surroundings;

b undertake studies that focus on geographical questions, e.g., 'What/

Where is it?' 'What is it like?', 'How did it get like this?', and that are based on direct experience, practical activities and fieldwork in the locality of the school; studies should involve the development of skills, and the development of knowledge and understanding about places and themes; and

c become aware that the world extends beyond their own locality, both within and outside the United Kingdom, and that the places they study exist within this broader geographical context, e.g., within a town, a region, a country.

## Geographical Skills

2 In investigating places and a theme, pupils should be given opportunities to observe, question and record, and to communicate ideas and information.
3 Pupils should be taught to:

b undertake fieldwork activities in the locality of the school, e.g., observing housing types, mapping the school playground;

## Places

5 In these studies, pupils should be taught:

a about the main physical and human features;
b how localities may be similar and how they may differ;
c about the effects of weather on people and their surroundings; and
d how land and buildings are used.

## Thematic Study

6 The quality of the environment in any locality, either in the United Kingdom or overseas, should be investigated. In this study, pupils should be taught:

a to express views on the attractive and unattractive features, e.g., tidiness, noise, of the environment concerned, e.g., a play area, a street, a small area of woodland;
b how that environment is changing, e.g., increasing traffic; and
c how the quality of that environment can be sustained and improved, e.g., creating cycle lanes, excluding cars from an area.

### Key Stage 2 Programme of Study

1 Pupils should be given opportunities to:

a investigate places and themes across a widening range of scales;
b undertake studies that focus on geographical questions, e.g., 'What/

where is it?', 'What is it like?', 'How did it get like this?', 'How and why is it changing?', and that involve fieldwork and classroom activities; studies should involve the development of skills, and the development of knowledge and understanding about places and themes;

c develop the ability to recognise patterns, e.g., variations in rainfall between places, patterns of land use in a settlement, and to apply their knowledge and understanding to explain them; and

d become aware of how places fit into a wider geographical context, e.g., links within a town, a rural area, a region.

*Geographical Skills*

3 Pupils should be taught to:

b undertake fieldwork, including the use of instruments to make measurements, and appropriate techniques.

*Places*

5 In these studies, pupils should be taught:

a about the main physical and human features, e.g., cliffs, valleys, housing estates, reservoirs, and environmental issues, e.g., water pollution, proposals for a new supermarket, that give the localities their character;

b how the localities may be similar and how they may differ;

c how the features of the localities influence the nature and location of human activities within them;

d about recent or proposed changes in the localities; and

e how the localities are set within a broader geographical context, and are linked with other places.

*Thematic Studies*

9 Settlement: In studying how settlements differ and change, pupils should be taught:

c about a particular issue arising from the way land is used, e.g., different groups of residents in a settlement have conflicting views on the construction of a by-pass across farmland.

10 Environmental change
In investigating how environments change, pupils should be taught:

a how people affect the environment, e.g., by quarrying, building reservoirs, building motorways; and b   how and why people seek to manage and sustain their environment, e.g., by combatting river pollution, by organic farming, conserving areas of beautiful landscape or of scientific value.

## The Place of Environmental Education in the Science Curriculum

*Key Stage 1 Programme of Study*

Pupils should be given opportunities to:

2   Science in everyday life

c   consider how to treat living things and the environment with care and sensitivity.

### Experimental and Investigative Science

Pupils should be taught:

1   Planning experimental work

a   to turn ideas suggested to them, and their own ideas, into a form that can be investigated;

2   Obtaining evidence

a   to explore using appropriate senses;
b   to make observations and measurements; and
c   to make a record of observations and measurements.

3   Considering evidence

### Life Processes and Living Things

Pupils should be taught:

2   Humans as organisms

f   that humans have senses which enable them to be aware of the world around them.

5   Living things in their environment

a   that there are different kinds of plants and animals in the local environment; and b that there are differences between local environments and that these affect which animals and plants are found there.

*Key Stage 2 Programme of Study*

Pupils should be given opportunities to:

2 Science in everyday life

d consider ways in which living things and the environment need protection.

**Experimental and Investigative Science**

Pupils should be taught:

1 Planning experimental work

a to turn ideas suggested to them, and their own ideas, into a form that can be investigated;

2 Obtaining evidence

a to use simple apparatus and equipment correctly;
b to make careful observations and measurements; and
c to check observations and measurements by repeating them.

3 Considering evidence

**Life Processes and Living Things**

Pupils should be taught:

5 Living things in their environment

*adaptation*
a that different plants and animals are found in different habitats; and
b how animals and plants in two different habitats are suited to their environment;
*feeding relationships*
c that food chains show feeding relationships in an ecosystem; and
d that nearly all food chains start with a green plant;
*micro-organisms*
e that micro-organisms exist, and that many may be beneficial, e.g., in the breakdown of waste, while others may be harmful, e.g., in causing disease.

*Joy Palmer*

## Notes

1   The following sources will be of practical assistance to those seeking help and
    advice for the task of designing and implementing a school policy document and
    related guidelines for environmental education in the primary school.

    NATIONAL ASSOCIATION FOR ENVIRONMENTAL EDUCATION (1992).
    NATIONAL CURRICULUM COUNCIL (1990a).
    NEAL, P.D. and PALMER, J.A. (1990).
    PALMER, J.A. and NEAL, P.D. (1994).

    *Also* publications of the Council for Environmental Education — publication list
    available from:
    CEE Information Unit
    University of Reading
    London Road
    Reading
    RG1 5AQ
    and publications of the National Association for Environmental Education — pub-
    lication list available from:
    NAEE
    University of Wolverhampton
    Walsall Campus
    Gorway
    Walsall
    WS1 3BD

## References

BACZALA, K. (1992) *Towards a School Policy for Environmental Education: An Environ-
    mental Audit*, NAEE, Walsall.
CEE (Council for Environmental Education) (1987) *Introducing Environmental Educa-
    tion; Book 2: Schools: Educating for Life*, Reading, CEE.
CURRICULUM COUNCIL FOR WALES (1991) *The Whole Curriculum 5–16 in Wales*, Cardiff,
    CWW.
DISINGER, J. (1983) 'Environmental education's definitional problem', *ERIC/SMEAC In-
    formation Bulletin No. 2*, Columbus, ERIC/SMEAC.
IUCN (International Union for Conservation of Nature and Natural Resources) (1970)
    *International Working Meeting on Environmental Education in the School Cur-
    riculum: Final Report*, September 1970, IUCN, New York.
IUCN, UNEP and WWF (1980) *The World Conservation Strategy*, New York.
IUCN, UNEP and WWF (1991) *Caring for the Earth: A Strategy for Sustainable Living*,
    New York.
NATIONAL ASSOCIATION FOR ENVIRONMENTAL EDUCATION (1992) *Statement of Aims and
    Objectives*, NAEE, Walsall.
NATIONAL CURRICULUM COUNCIL (1990a) *Curriculum Guidance 3: The Whole Curric-
    ulum*, York, NCC.
NATIONAL CURRICULUM COUNCIL (1990b) *Curriculum Guidance 7: Environmental Edu-
    cation*, York, NCC.
NEAL, P.D. and PALMER, J.A. (1990) *Environmental Education in the Primary School*,
    Basil Blackwell.

PALMER, J.A. (1993a) 'Development of concern for the environment and related formative influences of educators: A new research area in environmental education',
*Journal of Environmental Education*, **24**, 3, Washington, DC, pp.26–31.

PALMER, J.A. (1993b) 'From Santa Claus to sustainability: Emergent understanding of
concepts and issues in environmental science', *International Journal of Science
Education*, **15**, 5, pp.487–95.

PALMER, J.A. and NEAL, P.D. (1994) *The Handbook of Environmental Education*, London, Routledge.

STERLING, S. (1992) *A Short History of Environmental Education (to 1989)*, Walsall,
Staffs, National Association for Environmental Education.

UNCED (1992) *Agenda 21*, United Nations Conference on Environment and Development (The Earth Summit).

UNESCO (1978) *Final Report, Intergovernmental Conference on Environmental Education*, UNESCO with UNEP, Tbilisi, USSR.

WORLD COMMISSION ON ENVIRONMENT AND DEVELOPMENT (1987) *Our Common Future*,
OUP, Oxford, New York.

# Chapter 7

# Education for Citizenship

## Ian Davies

### Introduction

The 1990s, according to Sir Ralf Dahrendorf, will be 'the decade of the citizen' (Keane, 1990). Some valuable light has been shone on the meanings associated with the complex area of citizenship by Oliver and Heater (1994):

> Individuals are citizens when they practise civic virtue and good citizenship, enjoy but do not exploit their civil and political rights, contribute to and receive social and economic benefits, do not allow any sense of national identity to justify discriminating or stereotyping of others, experience a sense of non-exclusive multiple citizenship and, by their example, teach citizenship to others. (Oliver and Heater, 1994, p.8)

This chapter explores the meaning of education for citizenship and outlines some ways in which practical work can be undertaken. There are four main sections to the chapter: firstly, general comments are made on the nature of political learning in schools and the reasons for promoting different forms of that learning at different times; secondly, some of the main organizations which promote and investigate citizenship education are reviewed and recommendations by two of the most prestigious of those bodies are analysed; thirdly, a few examples of models of citizenship education are sketched; and finally practical suggestions are made based on a review of available literature and recent school practice.

### The Nature of Political Learning in Schools

Schools are always concerned, intentionally or otherwise, with political learning. The ways in which teachers manage classrooms, the respect that pupils have for rules, regulations and for each other, and many other features of what may be termed the hidden curriculum as well as the overtly political nature of what is studied, means that schools will always be one of the key locations for education for citizenship. The form of that learning however, varies greatly over time. During the last decade alone there have been at least three versions of political learning that have been emphasized by key politicians or educationalists. Firstly, political literacy was officially sanctioned at the end of the 1970s and into the early 1980s. It was concerned with developing pupils' skills and preparing them to take political action. It used the study of issues rather than institutions to develop those skills, and so was concerned with promoting a broad definition of politics. Secondly, various aspects of 'new' educations such as global education, peace education, development education and gender education, came to prominence from the early 1980s. This form of education is characterized by affective learning and holistic approaches to world issues. Dismissed by some (e.g., Scruton, 1985) as being a thinly veiled attempt at indoctrinating pupils it nevertheless has gained widespread recognition as a professional way forward and research evidence has shown that, especially in primary schools, it continues to be valued particularly for its emphasis on active, experiential learning (Vulliamy and Webb, 1993). Thirdly, education for citizenship is that form of political learning which is currently officially sanctioned. A crude overview would see it as that which emphasizes voluntary service in a society in which obligations are perhaps as, or more, important than rights.

It is important, however, to consider, generally at this stage, why the shifts from one sort of political learning to another have taken place. In the early 1970s the following factors were felt to be important for promoting political learning (Lister, 1985):

1   Research in the field of political socialisation revealed that young people possessed some knowledge of politics and so arguments that suggested that young people's innocence had to be preserved were weakened.
2   There was a growing concern for the democratisation of education systems.
3   The lowering of the age of majority and of the voting age meant that some young people would be voting while still at school.
4   School textbook research was part of the general concern for improved political education in schools.
5   Sociological studies of school political structures raised questions about the possible democratisation of those structures.
6   Suggestions of mass political ignorance based on various surveys led many to argue that a democracy founded on ignorance was a contradiction in terms.

Research in the early 1990s which sought to probe why education for citizenship was being promoted (Davies, 1992) led to the following very different factors being highlighted by respondents:

1   Demographic shifts mean that the same reliance cannot be placed on the welfare state and individuals need to become more active as citizens.

2  Ideological considerations have placed a greater emphasis on the individual rather than the community.

3  There has been a growth in the importance attached to consumers and consumerism which is very different from the earlier concern with issues relating to political power. Economics has supplanted politics.

4  A rising crime rate together with a weakened local government has led to the call for greater individual responsibility.

There are, however, a great many variants of education for citizenship on offer, and teachers are at least potentially likely to incorporate new reforms into existing ways of teaching rather than take on completely new ways overnight (Reynolds and Saunders, 1987).

### Organizations and Initiatives Associated with Education for Citizenship

Although it focuses predominantly on secondary education, the National Foundation for Educational Research provides an excellent summary of initiatives in this area (Taylor, 1992). There are a number of key organizations active in the field of which only two are briefly mentioned below.

The Centre for Citizenship Studies in Education is based at the University of Leicester. It was set up in 1991 in response to a recommendation of the Speaker's Commission on Citizenship. Research and development work is undertaken giving rise to a number of broadsheets and other material which is of use to teachers. A strong relationship with industry and commerce is in evidence.

The Citizenship Foundation is based in Charterhouse Street, London. Building on the work of the *Law in Education Project* it has a special interest in the law, critical thinking and moral stage theory. Its journal *Citizenship* is of use to teachers and others. Research has been undertaken and teaching materials have been produced and a recent project carried out in collaboration with the Home Office has led to the production of teaching materials specifically written for primary school pupils (Rowe and Newton, 1994). While the key ideas of rights, responsibilities and justice (fairness) permeate the materials, following an introduction, these are in five main sections, which are concerned with friendship, rules, property and power, respecting differences, and community and environment. Particular use is made of stories to raise moral dilemmas and conflicts to which children can relate and which will stimulate them to reflect upon their own experiences and in so doing develop through discussion alternative suggestions as to how these might be resolved. To give one example for children in Key Stage 1, in the section on friendship a story entitled 'Polly makes a move' focuses on a young girl who faces difficulties settling into a new school. Notes for teachers suggest questions that can be asked to stimulate discussion on issues — such as loneliness at playtime —

arising from the story and to encourage children to explore the nature of friendship. In addition to the above, there are many other organizations, projects and publications which are worth attention, and some of those are mentioned at the end of this chapter.

Two significant reports are seen as being very influential in contributing to the debate about education for citizenship. They will therefore be briefly analysed in turn. The first is *Curriculum Guidance 8: Education for Citizenship* which was produced by the now defunct National Curriculum Council (NCC) in 1990 as one of the five cross-curricular themes. The NCC's report states that schools should take the responsibility, along with others, to develop the knowledge, understanding, skills and attitudes needed to explore, make decisions about and exercise a range of rights and responsibilities in various local, national and international contexts. The NCC suggest eight 'essential components'. The first three explore broad areas: the nature of community; roles and relationships in a pluralist society, and the duties, responsibilities and rights of being a citizen. The remaining five explore specific everyday contexts for citizenship in the present and future lives of pupils: the family; democracy in action; the citizen and the law; work, employment and leisure; public services (NCC, 1990, p.5).

The NCC report fails to give a proper definition of a citizen; it omits to explain the differences between political and social citizenship; it does not discuss the relationship between rights and responsibilities; and it gives no indication that citizenship is itself a controversial issue. Care will have to be taken that an explicit consideration of politics is not simply allowed to disappear from lessons as has happened at times within the context of personal and social education (Fiehn, 1986). This point is particularly relevant when one notes that one commentator (Ward, 1990) interpreted the NCC to be suggesting that 'a specific study of politics should not begin until the age of 14' (p.4). The NCC report with its emphasis on a pluralist society is expressing a political preference. The recognition that the police service is of the 'greatest importance' (p.13), the status accorded to the virtues of wealth creation (p.9), the omission of issues surrounding wealth distribution, and the European dimension, the inability to use the word 'rights' without qualifying it in some way by referring to, for example, duties or privileges, all suggest that a traditional difficulty has emerged: substantive values may be promoted and a critical analysis of power may be neglected. Indeed it is an issue that those who follow the NCC report would perhaps be attempting to educate about a pluralist society that does not yet exist.

The second report to be analysed here has been produced by the Speaker's Commission and is entitled *Encouraging Citizenship*. Some of the main recommendations from the Commission are as follows:

> Every young person should study and experience citizenship from their earliest years through to higher education, whether in state or private school.

Charters and conventions on human rights should provide reference points within the classroom. Every school governing body should ask for a strategy for developing and monitoring citizenship across the curriculum.

Citizenship skills should be included in records of achievement.

Schools and colleges should be given a copy of the Speaker's Commission report.

Teachers, doctors, nurses, local government workers, police, armed forces, civil servants and judges should be given specific training on citizenship.

But the main way in which the Commission saw young citizens being active was through voluntary work. Wringe (1992) feels that there may be an exploitation of the ideals of youth in such a venture, and that it will also be ineffective:

voluntary activity is essentially patchy. It also deprives people of their rights, and their dignity, for what is done voluntarily cannot be demanded, and must be received with gratitude. It may also inhibit the provision of more reliable forms of relief. (Wringe, 1992, p.35)

In short, a coherent public health service is better than a 'Good Samaritan'. This is supported by research evidence which shows the rather low and uncertain level of involvement of people in voluntary activity (Papers for the Commission on Citizenship, no date).

## Models of Citizenship Education

It is, of course, necessary to go beyond recommendations and a description of the framework of documents, and to probe what this work by these high-status groups actually seeks to achieve. It is difficult, if not impossible, to produce any certainties as it is extremely difficult to define citizenship (Heater, 1990). It is interesting, though, that as a starting point the Speaker's Commission took the work of Marshall (1963) who wrote that:

Citizenship is a status bestowed on all those who are full members of a community. All who possess this status are equal with respect to the rights and duties with which the status is endowed. There are no universal principles that determine what those rights and duties shall be, but societies in which citizenship is a developing institution create an image of ideal citizenship against which achievement can be directed. The urge forward along the path thus plotted is an urge toward a fuller measure of equality, an enrichment of the stuff of which the status is made and an increase in the number of those upon whom the status is bestowed. . .Citizenship requires. . .a direct sense of community membership based on loyalty to a civilisation which is a common possession. It is a loyalty of free men endowed with rights and protected by a common law. Its growth is stimulated by the struggle to win those rights and their enjoyment when won (Marshall, 1963, pp.87 and 96).

Marshall is criticized by teachers for being an academic sociologist and not an educationalist, for his sexism which although probably not noticed at the time of writing is certainly not appropriate today; and for his failure, according to some, to place a sufficient emphasis on conflict and struggle. His outline of emerging rights and responsibilities related, mainly, to the law in the eighteenth century, politics in the nineteenth century and welfare in the twentieth century seems too straightforward. It seems at least in the outline given here to ignore both ancient conceptions which emerged from the Graeco-Roman world which focused on the concept of civic virtue and the good citizen; and the modern forms of citizenship which would encompass concerns with environmental matters, 'minority' groups, and dimensions which are more properly international.

The struggle over characterizations of citizenship is strongly fought. To give a crude overview of some views the following quotations show how there is a disagreement about whether to emphasize rights or responsibilities. For Douglas Hurd during his time as Home Secretary, when he was supported by a junior minister John Patten who later became Secretary of State for Education 'active citizenship is the free acceptance by individuals of *voluntary obligations* to the community of which they are members' (my emphasis) (Hurd, 1989, p.7). For the philosopher, novelist and broadcaster, Michael Ignatieff:

> The practice of citizenship is about ensuring everybody the entitlements necessary to the exercise of their liberty. As a political question welfare is about rights not caring. (Ignatieff, 1989, p.72)

Others, such as Carr (1991) have noted the broad range of differences within the citizenship debate by referring to market and moral models. For Carr the latter is intended to accommodate a broad range of democratic theories ranging from the classical theories of ancient Greece through the direct democracy of Rousseau, the developmental democracy of Mill, and the modern participatory theories of writers such as Pateman. The market model on the other hand is concerned with democracy as the most instrumentally effective system for protecting the freedom of individuals to pursue their private interests with minimal state interference.

Porter (quoted by Oliver and Heater, 1994, p.211) focuses on the three key elements of status, volition and competence. Although there are tensions between the key elements, he argues that status concerns the relationship of the citizen to the State which is often defined in the form of rights and duties by law. Volition is an affective category involving such things as feelings, inclinations and attitudes. Competence is the third area which allows citizenship to mean something for without a proper understanding of, for example, legal systems and the necessary skills to take action, status and volition would remain sterile.

The highly complex debate about the meaning of citizenship can be regarded positively. Education for citizenship is not something which is decided by experts and forced upon pupils. It should involve an exploration of key areas and lead to a situation in which young people are taking part in setting their own agendas and contributing constructively and critically to the development of a richer democratic society. Given this lofty aim and the complexities about the meaning of citizenship, it is necessary to sketch at least a few examples of the sort of classroom practice that can be employed.

## Examples of Practical Work for Teachers and for Pupils

Primary schools are very aware of the contribution that they make towards developing socially aware citizens who are sensitive to the needs of others. However, as acknowledged by Rowe and Newton (1994), making this explicit and setting out to plan and introduce a citizenship curriculum may prove difficult initially. They suggest the following starting points:

- response to narrative;
- response to short, 'clinical' dilemmas;
- response to illustration;
- response to the ideas of others in the class;
- reflection on personal experience;
- examination of elements of the social, moral, political, spiritual surrounding of pupils; and
- reflection through the use of individual writing (reflective or fictional), small group work, whole group discussion, role play or drama.

(Rowe and Newton, 1994, p.10)

There is much good work that can be done through the approach to classroom organization and the learning process adopted within topic or subject lessons. However, possibilities for citizenship education can be found within the content of the National Curriculum (see, for example, Davies (1994) writing about history) and within other cross-curricular themes (see, for example, Hooper (1993) writing about economic awareness).

A number of books have been published recently which are helpful to teachers seeking to explore interpretations of citizenship and identify opportunities for including it in the curriculum. More academic texts include those by Barbalet (1988); Heater (1990); Oliver and Heater (1994); Wright (1994);

Andrews (1991); Archard (1993); van Steenbergen (1994); Lynch (1992); and Turner (1993). Recent books which contain ideas but also focus on issues associated with implementation with practical examples include Conley (1991); Fogelman (1991); Baglin Jones and Jones (1992); Council for Education in World Citizenship (1992) and Edwards and Fogelman (1993). It may also be worth exploring some older texts which are related to citizenship. Here, both the classic statements (e.g., Dewey, 1966), as well as those which could be read with perhaps some amusement would illustrate how ideas have (hopefully) changed so dramatically (e.g., Hill, 1941). These books can be used for private reading but it is also fairly straightforward to use some of the sections from one or more of these publications so as to start a structured discussion on citizenship during an in-service session. In this respect the boxed quotations and case studies in the book by Oliver and Heater (1994) may prove to be particularly useful. Also, the checklists of questions provided by Lynch (1992) for reviewing policy and practice may give some prompts for staff discussion and whole-school evaluation.

It is important to note that Heater (1990) argues that one of the central concerns of citizenship is identity, and there are a number of straightforward exercises which can be employed ranging from an exploration of individual through to world identity. A good deal of material which can be used with pupils has been produced by those who emphasize the global education approach to citizenship (e.g., Pike and Selby, 1988). 'Ourselves', an extremely common topic in reception and Year 1 classes, can act as a vehicle for pupils not only to explore and develop a sense of their own worth but also to develop a heightened appreciation of the essential worth of others, a receptivity to perspectives different from their own and an understanding of the commonality of needs, rights and aspirations which characterizes us all.

At Key Stage 1 the school community is likely to provide a major focus for citizenship education. Identifying the roles, responsibilities and particular contribution of everyone, who works or participates in the life of the school, is a popular topic in infant classes. Analysing class activities in order to suggest helpful codes of behaviour is also well tried — for example, analysing group work, in order to better understand group dynamics and to identify which factors help or hinder cooperation. The establishment of better links with the local community in an attempt to develop pupils' capabilities for citizenship (Maxwell, 1994) can be very valuable. Surveys carried out to discover the attitudes of local people to aspects of road safety — such as the construction of a new pedestrian underpass — or the provision of amenities — such as the building of a new swimming pool — make interesting starting points. Classes who carry out exchanges with schools in contrasting localities in Britain or in other European countries have the opportunity to compare the nature and advantages and disadvantages of living in alternative communities.

Many secondary schools encourage children to manage a mock local, general or European election using resources from the Hansard Society and media organizations such as the BBC. Mock elections can also stimulate considerable interest and enthusiasm in primary schools, particularly at Key Stage 2. Pointers for consideration in holding such an election are as follows:

1 Have a clear rationale for the event and include learning objectives (for political learning and other aspects of the curriculum), activities, time allocation and method of evaluating the event in medium-term planning.
2 Explore with pupils the kinds and range of issues over which the election is to be fought and decide whether real and imaginary parties are to be represented. Brainstorm what is to be involved in the election process and on polling day and draw up an action plan and timetable.
3 Devise with pupils a simple system by which candidates will be chosen. For example, being proposed by a classmate, supported by two other pupils and producing a manifesto. Decide how candidates' campaign teams will be chosen/allocated and the kinds of activities in which they will be engaged.
4 Consider possibilities of developing a newsletter to report on the campaign and advertising posters. Campaign teams might also write publicity leaflets, hold meetings, address the school assembly, make tape recorded mock radio broadcasts and videos to simulate TV broadcasts. All of these activities provide valuable links with English, technology and media education.
5 Decide how the results will be presented and discussed. Identify a range of factors that teachers and pupils can use to evaluate the success of the election and the work of all involved — for example, criteria for a poster that attracts maximum attention and factors which promote a lively debate.

The value of school councils in primary schools, although still relatively rare, has been commented upon for their potential to develop communication skills, improve peer relationships, stimulate creativity and improve pupil behaviour and commitment to school (e.g., Haigh, 1994; Gorman, 1994; Siraj-Blatchford, 1995). Deciding how many representatives from each class might form the council, the qualities representatives might need, how they might be selected and the frequency of meetings provides an interesting and meaningful context for citizenship education. Also, as the issues which tend to be tackled — such as playground games and facilities, safe play, arrangements for wet playtimes, dinner time behaviour, girls' football or lack of it, school uniform and assemblies — have been identified for consideration because they affect the quality of the children's lives in school, the work of the council can have genuine relevance.

The hidden curriculum is always important, and there have been some interesting recent studies in relation to citizenship (e.g., John and Osborn, 1992). Children can be encouraged to identify the implicit rules operating within their class or throughout the whole school in order to discuss why these exist, what impact they have, where there are differences across the school and why, and whether any of these implicit rules should be challenged or made explicit. For example, through the use of pupil questionnaires, children have been assisted in reflecting on their own experience and identifying and opening up for discussion any sex-stereotyping or gender bias operating within their class or across the school.

The ways in which teachers manage discussions is linked to citizenship education. Rowe and Newton (1994) following Rowe (1994) have developed a threefold pedagogical model which relates to moral reasoning, philosophical enquiry and the development of empathy and a sense of community. The aim is to ensure that children are challenged in a systematic way to develop their thinking. In summary they suggest that the key points are:

- to encourage involved discussion from the maximum number of pupils;
- to use open-ended exploratory questions;
- to press children for reasons; and
- to discuss whether some actions are better than others.

In these ways this work would correspond closely to that which has been researched as leading to the achievement of higher order thinking (Newmann, 1990).

Many diverse and equally important areas compete for a space on the overcrowded INSET agenda of most primary schools. However, time set aside for the whole school to engage in informed discussion about citizenship can be enormously valuable in providing a basis of shared understanding and purpose from which to move forward. Detailed programmes of INSET material have been produced by a number of organizations. The Centre for Citizenship Studies in Education (Edwards, 1993) and various local education authorities are only two examples of bodies producing material.

The cooperative review of materials published for use as teaching aids can also be a very useful way to stimulate staff discussion and facilitate in-service work. There are vast amounts of classroom material available and lists can be found in Edwards (1993) and Rowe and Newton (1994). UNICEF has produced resources focusing on children's rights (UNICEF, 1990); Ian Addis (1992) has produced a thought provoking collection of stories; Joyce (1994) has a resource book concentrating on values education. While all these materials are intended to be used in primary schools, some of that which has been written for secondary schools may also be suitable for some children in Key Stage 2. The law is fully explored by the Law in Education project materials; and packs have been produced by both the Children's Society (no date) and a Birmingham consortium (Lloyd *et al.*, 1993) which may be of some value. Texts which show exercises for pupils include work by Aylett (1993) and Windsor (1993).

Link
with

It may be worthwhile to encourage teachers to know how to tackle opposition from colleagues who feel that citizenship education is the concern only of parents and friends rather than the school. Citizenship education is low status, it suffers from vague definition and, as it is controversial, teachers are open to accusations associated with bias and indoctrination. There are a number of strategies, which I have explored elsewhere (Davies, 1991), that can be employed to attempt to overcome these objections:

- the head, senior management team and governors should be targeted and convinced of the importance of citizenship education;
- teachers, parents and others should be made aware of central definitions of citizenship but encouraged to see the matter as capable of realization in a way that is appropriate to the local community;
- the presentation of initiatives is important and it may be necessary to stress that it is not one which is going to prove difficult for the school;
- the school's aims and schemes of work should be examined for areas of overlap with citizenship;
- flexible guidelines should be produced which have the support of key individuals and groups;
- the high status of the work should be stressed with reference to such bodies as the Speaker's Commission;
- attention should be drawn to research which recognizes the sensitivity and professionalism of teachers engaged in the handling of material which is not objective (e.g., Stradling, 1984); and
- above all, stamina in persuasiveness and a tactical awareness of when it is necessary to make concessions are important for getting such ventures off the ground.

## Conclusion

Education for citizenship is important and in a democratic society cannot be left to chance. It is quite properly one of the central concerns of professional educators and teachers are strongly encouraged to undertake work in this area by many official bodies. A wealth of material which can be employed in classrooms is readily available. The challenge for teachers and pupils is to be able to make sense of the complex conceptual, ideological, and political issues that dominate the field and then to develop clear and dynamic working patterns which facilitate the development of professional practice. At a time when primary schools may appear to be downplaying social goals in favour of individual achievement (Copeland, 1994), it is vital that the opportunities provided by the Dearing review of the National Curriculum are used in the best interests of all pupils. A daunting challenge, and yet one which can and should be met.

## References

ADDIS, I. (1992) *What Can the Matter Be?*, London, David Fulton.

ANDREWS, G. (Ed) (1991) *Citizenship*, London, Lawrence and Wishart.

ARCHARD, D. (1993) *Children: Rights and Childhood*, London, Routledge.

AYLETT, J.F. (1993) *The World of Citizenship*, London, Hodder and Stoughton.

BAGLIN JONES, E. and JONES, N. (1992) *Education for Citizenship: Ideas and Perspectives for Cross-curricular Study*, London, Kogan Page.

BARBALET, J.M. (1988) *Citizenship: Rights, Struggle and Class Equality*, Milton Keynes, Open University Press.

CARR, W. (1991) 'Education for citizenship', *British Journal of Educational Studies*, **39**, 4, pp.373–85.

CHILDREN'S SOCIETY (no date): *Education for Citizenship*, London, The Children's Society.

CONLEY, F. (Ed) (1991) *Political Understanding across the Curriculum*, London, Politics Association.

COPELAND, I. (1994) 'The primary school brochure: A sample analysis', *Educational Studies*, **20**, 3, pp.387–98.

COUNCIL FOR EDUCATION IN WORLD CITIZENSHIP (CEWC) (1992) *World Citizenship in the National Curriculum*, London, Council for Education in World Citizenship.

DAVIES, I. (1991) 'Citizenship: Some ideas for INSET', *Pastoral Care in Education*, **9**, 2, pp.22–5.

DAVIES, I. (1992) 'Guidelines for political education', D. Phil thesis, University of York.

DAVIES, I. (1994) 'Teaching and learning about interpretations of the recent European past for the purposes of developing European citizenship', *Discoveries*, **4**, pp.22–6.

DEWEY, J. (1966) *Democracy and Education*, London, The Free Press.

EDWARDS, J. (1993) *Cross-curricular theme pack 1: Citizenship*, Centre for Citizenship Studies in Education, University of Leicester.

EDWARDS, J. and FOGELMAN, K. (Eds) (1993) *Developing Citizenship in the Curriculum*, London, David Fulton.

FIEHN, J. (1986) 'The silent "P": Politics in PSE', *History and Social Science Teachers' Centre Review (ILEA)*, **6**, 2.

FOGELMAN, K. (1991) (Ed) *Citizenship in Schools*, London, David Fulton.

GORMAN, M. (1994) 'Education for citizenship', in VERMA, G.K. and PUMFREY, P.D. (Eds) *Cross-curricular Contexts, Themes and Dimensions in Primary Schools*, London, Falmer Press.

HAIGH, G. (1994) 'Voices of reason', *Times Educational Supplement*, 27 May.

HEATER, D. (1990) *Citizenship: The Civic Ideal in World History, Politics and Education*, London, Longman.

HILL, J.C. (1941) *Introduction to Citizenship*, Oxford, Oxford University Press.

HOOPER, G. (1993) *Citizenship: The Fraud Squad*, The Centre for Citizenship Studies in Education, University of Leicester.

HURD, D. (1989) 'Freedom will flourish where citizens accept responsibility', *The Independent*, 13 September.

IGNATIEFF, M. (1989) 'Citizenship and moral narcissism', *Political Quarterly*, **60**, 1, pp.63–74.

JOHN, P. and OSBORN, A. (1992) 'The influence of school ethos on pupils' citizenship attitudes', *Educational Review*, **44**, 2, pp.153–66.

JOYCE, S. (1994) *Values Education Resource Book*, London, Ginn.

KEANE, E. (1990) 'Decade of the citizen', *The Guardian*, 1 August.

LAW IN EDUCATION PROJECT (SCDC and Law Society) Parts 1–4 (1988–91) *Understand the Law*, London, Edward Arnold.

*Ian Davies*

Lister, I. (1985) *Political Education in England 1974–84*, Department of Educational Studies, University of York.

Lloyd, J., Nixon, J., Ranson, S., Baxter, A., Halsall, C., Pounce, E., Quinn, T. and Revill, R. (1993) *Democracy Then and Now*, London, Heinemann.

Lynch, J. (1992) *Education for Citizenship in a Multicultural Society*, London, Cassell.

Marshall, T.H. (1963) *Sociology at the Crossroads*, London, Heinemann.

Maxwell, E. (1994) 'Community building on the way up', *Times Educational Supplement*, 18 November.

National Curriculum Council (1990) *Curriculum Guidance 8: Education for Citizenship*, York, NCC.

Newmann, F. (1990) 'Qualities of thoughtful social studies classes', *Journal of Curriculum Studies*, **22**, 3, pp.253–75.

Oliver, D. and Heater, D. (1994) *The Foundations of Citizenship*, London, Harvester Wheatsheaf.

Papers for the Commission (no date) *Active Citizenship; A Review of the Research Evidence*, Speaker's Commission.

Pike, G. and Selby, D. (1988) *Global Teacher, Global Learner*, London, Hodder and Stoughton.

Reynolds, J. and Saunders, M. (1987) 'Teachers' responses to curriculum policy: Beyond the "delivery" metaphor', in Calderhead, J. (Ed) *Exploring Teachers' Thinking*, London, Cassell.

Rowe, D. (1994) *Moral Values and Citizenship: The Development of a New Programme for Primary Schools*, London, The Citizenship Foundation.

Rowe, D. and Newton, J. (1994) *You, Me, Us!*, London, The Home Office.

Scruton, R. (1985) *World Studies: Education or Indoctrination?*, London, Institute for European Defence and Strategic Studies.

Siraj-Blatchford, J. (1995) 'Little citizens: Helping children to help each other', in Siraj-Blatchford, J. and Siraj-Blatchford, I. (Eds) *Educating the Whole Child*, Buckingham, Open University Press.

Speaker's Commission on Citizenship (1990) *Encouraging Citizenship*, London, HMSO.

Stradling, R. (1984) *Teaching Controversial Issues*, London, Edward Arnold.

Taylor, M. (1992) *Citizenship Education in the UK: An Overview*, Slough, National Foundation for Educational Research.

Turner, B.S. (Ed) (1993) *Citizenship and Social Theory*, London, Sage.

UNICEF (1990) *The Rights of the Child*, UK, UNICEF.

van Steenbergen, B. (Ed) (1994) *The Condition of Citizenship*, London, Sage.

Vulliamy, G. and Webb, R. (1993) 'Progressive education and the National Curriculum: Findings from a global education research project', *Educational Review*, **45**, 1, pp.21–41.

Ward, D. (1990) 'Pupils should learn citizenship', *The Guardian*, 20 November.

Windsor, G. (1993) *Examining Citizenship*, London, Heinemann.

Wringe, C. (1992) 'The ambiguities of education for active citizenship', *Journal of Philosophy of Education*, **26**, 1, pp.29–38.

Wright, T. (1994) *Citizens and Subjects: An Essay on British Politics*, London, Routledge.

# Chapter 8

# Media Education: A Rich Life in the Margins

*Ken Fox*

If the curriculum is viewed as a landscape then we have endured the equivalent of several Ice Ages over the past five years. The development of a common National Curriculum has meant some subjects have been relocated in the margins and along the borderlines of curriculum priority. As a person of romantic sensibilities I quite like the idea of being seen as a curriculum renegade. However, in this chapter, mixing a little pragmatism with my romantic notions, I will outline a number of ways in which a rich life can be had in the margins, especially at a time when teachers are suffering from curriculum change fatigue.

We are all aware of the gaps that exist between curriculum laws that are handed down and what actually happens in the classroom. It is in these gaps, these curriculum breathing spaces, that subjects with the cross-curricular potential of media education can provide a unifying force. The pleasure, relevance and enthusiasm that is so important for teachers as well as pupils can be supplied through media education. The Dearing Review of the National Curriculum (SCAA, 1994) recommends that curriculum space should be found:

- to release the equivalent of a day a week of curriculum time in Key Stages 1 to 3 for schools to use at their own discretion;
- to increase flexibility in the Key Stage 4 curriculum.

(Dearing, 1993, p.12)

If, as the Dearing Report proposes, 'schools should be free to make their own decisions on how to achieve the required breadth and balance at each Key Stage', then a great opportunity exists for those areas such as media education to make a claim for inclusion in these curriculum gaps. Media education is centrally concerned with texts of the visual, audio, print and computer varieties, how they are constructed and how audiences understand them. There now seems to be acceptance in National Curriculum documents, the recent Orders for English being a prime example that the word 'text' refers to image based as well as print based communication. Media texts are used by teachers in all subjects, for example, as an illustration of Scotland in geography, or the photographs Key Stage 1 children are often asked to bring in as part of their topics on 'growth' or 'ourselves'. A media education approach would encourage teachers to look at how topic work or geography is constructed in these texts. Media education through the curriculum as a critical strategy with all texts is one way of ensuring a unified approach to the whole curriculum.

Ideally, I would like to see media education at the heart of a twenty-first century curriculum but in the short term it will operate at primary school level, in Key Stage 1, as an implicit suggestion about broadening the range of texts young children can explore in developing their literacy competencies. Key Stages 2, 3, and 4 English offer explicit proposals for using a range of media texts to develop the child's oral and written abilities. In Key Stages 3 and 4 media education has a parallel existence, as a separate examinable subject in the form of media studies, and the possibility of cross-curricular integration as a theme.

The following activities will focus on the development of media education as a cross-curricular theme within Key Stages 1 and 2. I hope the activities described will have the potential to be used by teachers from nursery to post-compulsory education. The audience I have in mind for this chapter is the teacher or the student teacher who wants to find out what media education is and how it can be used in the classroom as a cross-curricular theme. Media education might just supply the antidote to lift those curriculum fatigue blues.

## What Is Media Education?

In 1989, the year that has been renamed the 'year of responses' in National Curriculum circles, a Curriculum Statement produced by the British Film Institute National Working Party for Media Education, made up of teachers, inspectors, advisers, and lecturers, chaired by Cary Bazalgette of the BFI, offered a description of media education that has become the standard used by most subsequent publications in the field. This description was slightly modified for the publication of the *Secondary Curriculum Statement* (Bowker, 1991). I will merge these descriptions in the following quotation and then comment on the constituent parts I believe require further elaboration:

> Media education in the primary and secondary school seeks to increase children's understanding and enjoyment of the media — including television, film, video, radio, photography, popular music, printed materials, books, comics, magazines and the press, and computer software.

The issues that media education addresses are:

- how media texts work
- how they produce meaning

- how media institutions and industries are organised
- how audiences make sense of media products, technologies and institutions.

Media education aims to develop systematically children's critical and creative powers through analysis of media artefacts. This will deepen their knowledge and understanding of the pleasure and entertainment provided by the media. Media education aims to create more active and critical media users who will demand and, could contribute to, a greater range and diversity of media products. (Bowker, 1991, pp.1,2)

While these paragraphs beg many questions about pedagogy, organization, assessment and resourcing, both Curriculum Statements go on to present an accessible and teacher-friendly approach to providing answers. These documents represent the best starting point for teachers, advisers and student teachers who wish to develop their knowledge of what media education has to offer in theoretical and practical terms. Media education it is stated. . .'seeks to increase children's understanding and enjoyment of the media': it is important to note the emphasis on the affective as well as the cognitive domain. Media education can provide the opportunity for marrying in a dynamic but very natural way children's intellectual, practical and emotional concerns and questions. It is the emphasis on the interwoven nature of the analytical and the practical approaches that creates space for children to become reflective practitioners. As I shall demonstrate through the workshop examples I suggest, practical work in media education need not be overlooked because of the absence of video cameras or an editing suite from your resource budget. The low-tech approach does not mean that this is my preferred way of operating, but it does reflect the situation in many schools where media education does not feature in the curriculum, particularly at primary school level. It is important to be able to get started on media education with the resources that are available in the school.

### Rationale for Teaching about the Media

With the twenty-first century promising dramatic changes in media and communication technologies the media will play an even greater role in children's lives than it does at present. Using the argument of sheer quantity alone, it is blindingly obvious — so no doubt easily overlooked — that if we are in the business of educating children in preparation for life, then the curriculum must acknowledge the importance of education about the media. While media education might remain in the margins of the curriculum the media will become more central to children's lives. The range of employment opportunities available to school leavers will be reflected in the growth of the media and communications industries. The curriculum entrepreneurs cannot fail to see the potential in having a media literate population.

While the quantitative argument will probably run into difficulty over the question of what is worthy of study, I would like to offer a related rationale which emphasizes the importance of children's culture and touches on a larger discussion about what constitutes culture. The 'who is best?' debate about Bob Dylan or John Keats misses the point completely. They both form a part of the cultural heritage that exists for the twenty-first century child and both merit attention in their related fields. If schooling is to reach the children of this audiovisual age then it must address the totality of children's cultural experience. The investment made by many children in their media habits and tastes needs to be validated in the classroom. When I was of school going age I may have been on the register as the son of James and Rita Fox, but among my peers where it really mattered, I was identified by the team I supported, the collection of stickers I possessed and swapped with cut-throat skill, my favourite television programmes (for the nostalgia seekers among you, they were *The Time Tunnel* and *Voyage to the Bottom of the Sea*) and the dog-eared selection of comics I could purloin from my big brother's collection. The media products may be different for today's children but the strength of classroom culture remains fairly constant. The teacher can do a great deal to promote a child's self-concept by utilizing the range of media knowledge and understanding they bring to school. I am not suggesting that the classroom should be dominated by comics and computer games, or that teachers should invade children's culture in an inauthentic way, but the children's knowledge of story structure could be systematically developed through contact with a range of media texts that might include computer games, comics or favourite videos. The production by the children of a photo-story, comic, storyboard or video would encourage them to return to their own viewing experiences with a critical understanding promoted through practice and theory.

## Media Education: Key Concepts and the Development of Critical Thinking

Having outlined what media education is and why it should be part of the curriculum, I will now discuss how media education is structured conceptually. Rather than introduce these concepts as a set of new terms, I usually confront my B.Ed or in-service groups with a single image, or a short extract from a film and generate the 'who?' 'why?' 'how?' and 'for whom?' questions from discussion of the texts. Once they have used their own language to think about these texts conceptually I then introduce the diagram below.

1  Media texts
   • What does this text say?
   • How does it say it?
   • What sort of text is it?
2  Producers/audiences

- How was the text produced?
- By whom, and why, was it produced?
- For whom was it produced?
- How is it circulated to its audience?

3   Representations
- How do we judge the relation between media representation of people, places and events and their existence in the 'real' world?
- Who is included in these representations?
- Who is absent?

These three explanatory frameworks draw the key areas of knowledge and understanding in media education together. This model of the conceptual structure is developed in a very useful and influential book by Cary Bazalgette, *Teaching English in the National Curriculum: Media Education* (1991, p.19).

Each framework provides the basis for examining media products and suggesting ways in which practical work could be generated from the initial analysis. The workshop activities that follow take each of the frameworks as their starting point focusing on work within English, art, geography, environmental studies, design and technology. The questions that underpin this analytical/practical approach are truly cross-curricular in that they promote critical thinking about the media and its role in our lives. Empowering students to ask questions should be a central goal of any school curriculum, but as the 'centre' often does not hold with questioning approaches it leaves more space for those of us in the margins to fulfil that role.

## Turning Theory into Practice: Image Analysis

A group of Key Stage 1 children sit around a table with their teacher talking about photographs of themselves when they were babies as part of their topic work on growing up. How often have I seen images being used in this way. Generally the talk is very animated as each child tries to define their presence through that photographic evidence of themselves. Perhaps the teacher will have brought in a photograph of herself as a baby. From such a common place activity media education can develop. The purpose of these activities is to encourage audiences to look more closely at the array of images that surround them in their everyday lives. The ubiquity of the photographic image makes it an ideal starting point for work in media education. One of the best and cheapest resources any teacher or training teacher can collect is a store of photographic images. A box file or large envelope full of images from magazines, newspapers, catalogues, snap-shots, postcards, brochures, prospectuses, can supply the raw material for in-depth image analysis, photo-story production, collage or wall display. If you live near a local newspaper it is worth enquiring what they do with the photographs they take but don't publish. As the originals are kept on negative for easier storage, many of the good quality black and white prints are destroyed. They may be willing to let you have some of this material for little or no charge and these images, because they are of a high quality, can be photocopied and recycled in a variety of ways. Taking an image from one of the sources mentioned above, these are the questions that will help to structure the work I go on to outline.

## Media Texts

What does this text say? How does it say it? What sort of text is it? If it is a photograph from a newspaper then it will normally be accompanied by a headline or caption. What the image says will largely be determined by the words that anchor the meaning of the photograph. If you remove the accompanying words and present the photograph alone then the audience will be inclined to supply their own caption or headline. Once they know that the photograph is from a newspaper they will have expectations about how to read and interpret the image and what range of words they could employ with the image. These questions can be explored further by gathering a range of photographs with their captions or headlines from a variety of sources. Separate the words from the pictures, making a note of the original combinations. Place the words in one envelope and the photographs in another and ask your students to match them. What usually emerges is that it is possible to match the words with a whole variety of images other than the original combinations. What this activity makes clear is the ambiguous nature of the image and the way images are constructed to suit an audience and an intention. With photographs being used as evidence in a whole range of media texts from newspapers to school books it is important that students are encouraged to look more closely at how the image is produced. This leads directly to the second explanatory framework in media education focusing on the producers and the audiences.

## Producers and Audiences

How was the text produced? By whom, and why, was it produced? For whom was it produced? How is it circulated to its audiences?

These questions encourage the development of practical work in putting the pupils at the centre of the production process. They should be given the opportunity to take their own photographs. The resource implications need not be an inhibiting factor. Many pupils own their own cameras or have access to a camera from home, and there are many relatively cheap ways of getting film processed. Working with younger pupils it would be possible to start them off with a framing device that they cut out of card. This framing device can be used to simulate the camera viewfinder and allow younger pupils to sustain and develop the visual vocabulary you would have begun to introduce using the large store of still images mentioned earlier. Idealistic though it may sound, it is often remarkable how very young children use these photographs to explore aspects of their own identity. Searching for images of young people in newspapers or magazines makes one realize that very few positive images are circulated. Like many other less powerful groups in our society children rarely have a say in how images of them are produced and how they are represented in these available images.

For young people, the production of their own images of themselves can be a significant development in their self-esteem and their awareness of how other minority groups are represented.

*Representations*

How do we judge the relation between media representations of people, places and events and their existence in the 'real' world. Who is included in these representations? Who is absent?

A way to explore this aspect of media education through image analysis is to ask the pupils to bring in examples of their most recent birthday cards. In a class of 10-year-old boys and girls the images that adorn these cards will supply a rich resource for investigating who is represented and who is not. From a detailed study of the cards, the colours, images, motifs, words and dress sense of the children depicted, it becomes clear that what is on offer is an idealized version of children and childhood produced by adults. If the children look around the classroom it is unlikely that the images on offer represent who they are, or how they would like to be portrayed. The pupils move into practical mode by producing their own images, through photography or drawing and using these on the cover of birthday cards. Images by children of children for children.

## Theory into Practice: Soap Operas and Sense of Place

This workshop is based on a range of classroom activities developed in primary and secondary schools. It combines work on the media, English, geography, design and technology, environmental awareness and personal and social education. Developing spatial awareness and a sense of *the place* children call home, school, the town, the city, the country, the beach, is a fundamental feature of children's growing knowledge of the world. The various syllabuses in maths, science, English, geography, history, art, design and technology cover some aspects of the knowledge, understanding and skills related to this area. Media education can be used to present a coherent blend of analytical and practical work based on this theme. Schools do their best to foster a sense of community, but in today's fragmented post-industrial world where do we get most of our images of community life? The opening title sequences of a number of British or Australian soap operas do their utmost to locate the audience in a specific place. The resource you will need to set this work in motion is a set of opening title sequences of five or six current soap operas on video-tape. I am not suggesting that the communities on view in soap operas offer the only model of community life but they are all-pervasive and inhabit our cultural world in a complex and useful way. The three explanatory frameworks in media education provide the unifying structure for the analytical/practical approach to this theme. Beginning with questions of soap operas as media texts ensures questions of audiences, producers and representations will inevitably arise.

### Soap Operas as Media Texts

What type of text is it? What does this text say? How does it say it?

Identifying the type of text it is will not prove difficult for many pupils, but a cry of cultural heresy may arise from some of the teachers. The use of the soap opera for classroom analysis allows the teacher to make links between the tradition of nineteenth-century writing developed by Charles Dickens, with his cliff-hanger endings and multiplicity of story lines, and the rich tradition of storytelling of which soap opera is a modern equivalent providing audiences with the pleasures of continuous narrative. The ongoing nature of the story means that serious social issues can be dealt with over a longer period of time and not sensationalized to fit in with the two minute report they are given on the news. The enormous popularity of *Coronation Street, EastEnders, Neighbours, Home and Away, Emmerdale* and *Brookside*, suggest these texts possess a combination of elements to which people respond. The students are asked to list the storytelling conventions used in soap operas. These might include: the cliff-hanger; the multiplicity of story lines and characters; the relationships between characters; the use of a central location; the emphasis on dialogue; the frequency and duration of the soap stories; and the need to bring some stories to a conclusion while others simmer under the surface. The production of a character map will reveal the relationships between characters and how much of the action is based in and around the family, in whatever way the family is constructed. As soon as there is a recognition of the theme tune audiences have certain expectations about what is to follow. These expectations arise out of the audience's awareness of the genre, and their familiarity with the conventions and stylistics used in this form of storytelling. The concept of genre has cross-curricular appeal as it is essential in developing children's understanding of how to interpret and discuss texts in a variety of different subjects. A close analysis of the opening title sequences reveals a concentration on graphics and images associated with spatial awareness. Maps, street furniture, street signs, landmarks, and the movement from the establishing shots of the city, to the specific area known as Coronation Street, Brookside Close or Ramsey Street, all contribute with the theme music and the regular time of viewing to promote a strong sense of place. The emphasis on the development of pupils' knowledge and understanding of *place* in Key Stages 2 and 3 geography suggests that the uncovering of this shared knowledge about soap operas could be the source for extended work on mental mapping, map making, and local studies. Key Stage 1 children can be involved in this work as for many of them the first place they really get to know outside the home is the school. In fact, for many very young children who live in areas where they have little direct access to safe and secure playing facilities, the school space becomes their most important site for the development of spatial awareness.

The questions of who is represented in soap opera opening titles and who is absent could also be used by the children to investigate the images of their own community that students see in school or college prospectuses, local authority publications, and in the local and national press. The major practical work in this area would emerge from the earlier analysis of the soap opera opening titles when the pupils are asked to develop their own opening title sequence for a story about their classroom, school, locality or community. The children take on the role of producers and they construct a sequence of still or video images to represent their school/locality/community to outside audiences. Giving pupils the opportunity to identify the ten or twelve key images they would use to represent their place is very revealing about what they think is important in terms of facilities, meeting points, and other social spaces. How would you make an audience from Bath aware that this story about your place is set in Canterbury? What signs, symbols or maps would you include? This workshop takes the knowledge students already possess, systematically develops their understanding and involves them in practical skills that have cross-curricular pay-offs in the subjects identified earlier.

### Media Education's Sense of Place in the Curriculum

How and where will space be found for media education *through* the curriculum? The curriculum guidance offered in the National Curriculum Council document on *The Whole Curriculum* (NCC, 1990) provides a useful set of models for coping with the freeing up of non-core teaching time. A curriculum audit would allow the teachers, governors, parents and pupils to agree on how cross-curricular elements such as media education could be incorporated. Involving primary school pupils in this process may seem ambitious but part of the strength of media education is the way it can help to develop the knowledge and understanding the children bring with them to school. Media education helps to identify the home as a site for meaning making where the children have most of their contact with the media. At a curriculum review meeting the place of media education as a cross-curricular theme could be questioned and developed. There are, of course, staffing, training and resource implications that need to be given priority to ensure any cross-curricular theme

Ken Fox

is developed and sustained. If a media education approach is to be fostered in schools to help children of the twenty-first century become more critical and creative consumers and producers of media products, a systematic programme of in-service support needs to be made available. The support material for such a programme currently exists in the form of an excellent in-service package devised by the British Film Institute and the Open University. *Media Education: An Introduction* (BFI, 1992), would be an ideal resource for any school planning to develop media education as a cross-curricular theme.

Apart from its recognized site within English, the British Film Institute's response to the recently produced National Curriculum Orders (Bowker, 1994, pp.1–5) identifies media education at Key Stages 1 and 2 in information technology, history, art, and geography curriculum orders. Information technology with its emphasis on visual, print and aural forms has direct links with practical media education. 7-year-olds using a CD-Rom will be engaged in developing skills, knowledge and understanding related to media education. In the new orders for history at Key Stage 1 provision is made for pupils to 'identify different ways in which the past is represented, e.g., pictures, films, television programmes etc.'; the work I outline in the first workshop on image analysis deals directly with questions of representation. At Key Stage 2 the coverage of Victorian Britain and Britain Since 1930 would be enhanced by using media artefacts both as 'evidence' and as 'constructions' of popular culture. The development of cinema from the optical toys of the Victorian era to Hollywood blockbusters of today could form the basis for an exciting cross-curricular project, especially as the centenary of cinema is currently being celebrated. The development of 'visual literacy' in art at all Key Stages has a direct tie-in with work in media education. In the core subjects of science and maths, work on the design and basic principles of animation, photography, sound and music, could provide a strong link with art, design and technology, information technology and media education. As we approach the twenty-first century the influence of the media on all our lives will undoubtedly increase. Therefore, it is essential to ensure that children's critical and creative abilities for dealing with the media through media education are developed in all aspects of the curriculum. Media education's distinctive conceptual structure, with the emphasis on theory being informed by practice and subject matter which is so closely bound up with the totality of children's cultural experience could help to provide some of the breadth and balance the child, the teacher and the curriculum need.

**References**

BAZALGETTE, C. (1991) *Teaching English in the National Curriculum: Media Education*, London, Hodder.
BOWKER, J. (Ed) (1991) *Secondary Media Education: A Curriculum Statement*, London, BFI Education.

BOWKER, J. (Ed) (1994) *National Curriculum Orders: Response from the British Film Institute*, London, BFI Education.
DEARING, R. (1993) *The National Curriculum and its Assessment: Final Report*, London, SCAA.

## Resources

The following curriculum resources and books offer the most useful guides to classroom practice and curriculum planning in media education.

BRITISH FILM INSTITUTE (BFI) (1992) *Media Education: An Introduction*. London, Open University Press.

A comprehensive in-service package with audio and video resources, a teacher's workbook and a reader with articles on classroom practice, the development of media education, and its links with other areas of the curriculum. Available from the BFI Education Department at a cost of £80 (approx.). Making contact with the BFI Education Department at 21 Stephen Street, London W1P 1PL (071 255 1444) to request their catalogue of educational materials and a possible contact name of an inset provider in your area would be an excellent way to start the development of school resources for media education.

Essential books to help you get started:

BAZALGETTE, C. (Ed) (1989) *Primary Media Education: A Curriculum Statement*, London, BFI.
BAZALGETTE, C. (1991) *Media Education: Teaching English in the National Curriculum*, London, Hodder.
BOWKER, J. (Ed) (1991) *Secondary Media Education: A Curriculum Statement*, London, BFI.
BUCKINGHAM, D. (Ed) (1990) *Watching Media Learning*, London, Falmer Press.
BUCKINGHAM, D. (1993) *Children Talking Television*, London, Falmer Press.
CRAGGS, C. (1993) *Media Education in the Primary School*, London, Routledge.
HARPLEY, A. (1991) *Bright Ideas in Media Education*, Scholastic.
REID, M. (1993) *Main Street*, Glasgow/London, Scottish Film Council British Film Institute.
(An excellent resource for Key Stage 1 teachers which helps to develop young children's awareness of sense of place through still and moving images.)

*Chapter 9*

# Developing a School's Work with its Parents: Key Task or Optional Extra?

*John Bastiani*

During the last decade, relations between parents and their children's schools have undergone profound changes. One does not have to go back far to find a period in which all that was formally required from teachers in this area was a rather minimal commitment, intermittent contact and almost entirely one-way traffic! Of course many schools, supported by committed LEAs, went much further than this. The post-war growth of 'good practice', through more effective home–school communication and through the involvement of par-ents in the life and work of their children's schools, has been both varied and successful, especially in the primary phase.

But this was largely work inspired by a commitment to a wider view of schooling, which is concerned more broadly with children's developmental needs and with their everyday experience in real communities, as well as by growing evidence of the tangible benefits that practical cooperation between families and schools could bring. It continued to be, however, an essentially optional extra, rather than a formal requirement. It is only in recent years that the development of a school's work with its parents has become, as the con-sequence of a series of government interventions, legal requirements and administrative 'recommendations', an inescapable task for all schools and all teachers.

This chapter sets out to consider the impact of this massive shift of em-phasis upon the work of schools and teachers, against the background of:

- the continuing and often contradictory interest of politicians, of all kinds in parents as a constituency;
- the widespread recognition of the diversity and the considerable achievements of evidence and 'good practice' in the home–school area; and
- the steadily growing sense amongst parents of their entitlement to be fully accepted as important figures in their children's education with a key role to play. This is increasingly matched by a willingness to pursue this actively through their children's schools and through membership of a growing number and range of parent initiatives and organizations.

*Table 9.1: Parents and their children's schools: A summary of new legal requirements since 1980*

| | |
|---|---|
| 1980 | Right to express a preference for children's school.<br>Information about curriculum and organization of school. |
| 1981 | Right to participate in assessment of special needs. |
| 1986 | Increased parental representation on governing bodies.<br>Annual governors report at special meeting. |
| 1988 | Open enrolment for schools.<br>Information about children's programme of work and their progress.<br>Right to vote on opting out of LEA control. |
| 1989 | Children's Act gives priority to child's welfare.<br>Rights and responsibilities for parents. |
| 1991 | The Parent's Charter. |
| 1992 | Parents to be consulted before the formal inspection of a school. |
| 1993 | Annual ballots on grant-maintained status. |
| 1994 | New Code of practice on special educational needs assessment.<br>School attendance offences.<br>Lay-people on education appeal committees. |

But even this is not the whole picture. For at the very same time that schools are wrestling with the task of reviewing their experience in this area and attempting to develop appropriate professional attitudes and skills, relevant policies and effective practice, government policies have led to savage and progressive cuts in the provision of staff with specialist responsibilities who have already contributed enormously to home–school work.

Home–school liaison projects have, over the years, provided a body of professionals, (usually, but not always, with classroom teaching backgrounds) who have acquired knowledge, skill and experience through their specialist roles. These include home visiting, family learning sessions, running parent groups of various kinds, outreach work, working with community organizations and with a range of other agencies.

This work, funded partly from mainstream LEA budgets, but especially through the Urban Programme, City Challenge, GEST 'Raising Pupils' Standards in Inner Cities' and Section 11 work with minority ethnic pupils and families has supported much home–school liaison work whose very existence is now under threat. This applies particularly to key strategies which require considerable staff time and effort, such as visiting the homes of new and prospective pupils, or running a parents' support group. Ironically, such work raises, in a peculiarly heightened way, the question of how such work can be tapped by 'mainstream' schools and teachers and become 'embedded' in their everyday life and work — across phases and in all types of school situations.

During the last fifteen years, successive Conservative governments have introduced a series of legal requirements (see Table 9.1) which have introduced a cumulative number of rights, entitlements and, more recently, obligations, for parents/carers of children in maintained schools of all kinds. To get a better sense of perspective, these (often far-reaching) changes need to be understood against a wider background which has seen the introduction of the

National Curriculum, new patterns of assessment, devolved budgets, open enrolment and new arrangements for the formal inspection of schools. Most readers will not need to be reminded of this!

The political agenda underlying these developments could be seen to have two dimensions. The first, for which there currently seems to be broad cross-party consensus and support, derives from the following areas of concern:

- Clarification of rights and obligations in line with the rising expectations of parents (and pupils) and the strengthening of their rights and entitlements through improved access or negotiated agreements;
- Provision of information about children's programmes of work, about the curriculum and organization of schools and about changes in the education system;
- Provision of evidence of performance to parents about their children and, through the publication of comparative data, to enable them to compare teachers and schools; and
- Building and strengthening accountability through effective governing bodies.

The second, which gives much of the legislation its characteristic flavour, derives from a narrowly focused consumerism, which separates providers (schools) from consumers (parents). This is situated within an ideological commitment and a harsh application of market values in which a combination of opting out of LEA control and competition for places in popular schools will 'drive up standards'. Leaving aside the merits of such a view there is, it has to be said, no evidence that this has, or is likely to, happen.

The focal point of government policy in this area, has been the two versions of 'The Parent's Charter' ('91 and '94) which combines elements of the two overlapping versions of political interest through its development of parents 'right to know' and through five key documents:

- a report about your child;
- regular reports from independent inspectors;
- a performance table for your local schools;
- a prospectus or brochure about individual schools; and
- an annual report from your school's governors.

(DES, 1991, p.2)

## Competition Versus Cooperation

The legacy of the present Government's interest in parents' relationships with their children's schools is now becoming clear. For whilst there have been some benefits in the refocusing of efforts in this area, such as a growing sense of parental entitlement to information about their children's work and progress, the overall effects seem to be negative and unhelpful — in particular:

- most of the comparisons that are made between schools are unfair and not valid;
- 'parental choice' leads to a spurious overconcern with a school's image, rather than the underlying realities and the problems which schools inevitably face;
- open enrolment is destroying the special relationships between schools and the communities which they serve, which have often been a key part of their special ethos and identity, in which education can be more genuinely related to the lives and experiences of pupils and their families, and in which schools are regarded as a community resource;
- above all, a competitive model of schooling, in which consumers and providers are separated, precludes a view of education in which
  families and schools *work together*,
  parents and teachers are *both* educators — working in different ways and in different settings; and
  responsibility for children's learning is *shared* through practical cooperation and partnership involving teachers, parents, and, increasingly as they get older, pupils themselves.

### Why Home–School Relations Matter

Parents are a child's first, and most important, educators. Families are the biggest influence upon children's attitudes, behaviour and achievements. This is not surprising when one considers that children spend less than 15 per cent of their lives between birth and 16 in school and 85 per cent as the responsibility of parents and other carers.

What is, perhaps, less well-known is that families *continue* to be a crucial influence upon children as they get older and pass through the system. The work of people like Mortimore *et al.* (1988) and Goldstein (1991) has been seminal in this area. Finding appropriate ways in which the continuing interest, involvement and support of parents of older pupils can be maintained has become a necessary and challenging task. The implications for secondary schools are striking here.

Whilst parents are of first importance, schools, in the words of a famous study, '*do* make a difference'. Even when important initial differences are taken into account, some schools are very much better than others at getting the best from their pupils. In all cases 'effective schools' work well with their parents and are striving to become even better. More specifically, this means:

- developing more effective ways of communicating about the life and work of the school in ways appropriate to its parents;

- providing a range of opportunities for parents to become actively involved in their children's schooling;
- a recognition of the role of parents as educators themselves and a practical ability to capitalize on their influence; and
- generating a sense of common enterprise, based upon shared responsibility and joint action.

Recent legislation, too, has directed attention to the importance of working with parents. All maintained schools are now required to report to parents on their children's progress, to provide information on their programmes of work, to include parent representation on governing bodies, and to hold an annual meeting for all parents to discuss the governors' report. Additionally schools are now required to include work with parents in their development plans, and the formal inspection of schools must be preceded by a specially arranged parents' meeting.

Finally, there is abundant evidence that practical cooperation between families and schools works. Long established schemes, such as Portage, IMPACT Maths, and home-reading schemes show clearly that, when parents, teachers and pupils work together, the benefits are immediate, tangible and lasting.

## Funded Home–School Initiatives and Programmes

In a recently updated and extended publication, the 'UK Directory of Home–School Initiatives', the present author has brought together information about a wide range of very different initiatives (including those mentioned above) in England and Scotland, which are variously resourced through a variety of government, LEA, and, increasingly mixed funding. This has the effect of raising the profile of such work. It also provides an opportunity to learn some lessons from what is often very well established and highly developed work.

Inevitably, entries reflect some of the present preoccupations of such schemes. These include a number of concerns which link up with the themes of this chapter, such as:

- a willingness to consider and develop guidelines, frameworks and policies;
- making the enhanced experience of project schools more generally available to a bigger audience through wider dissemination strategies;
- a sharper emphasis on the achievements of such work, through better monitoring, inspection and evaluation arrangements; and
- a greater impact and take-up of ideas and practices in all schools through the greater availability of INSET and professional development activities.

### Partnership with Parents: Empty Rhetoric or Practical Goals?

Without doubt, the dominant metaphor of home–school liaison and parental involvement in their children's schooling has been that of 'partnership'. At worst, this can be caricatured as a fixed, ideological state of utopian bliss. At best, partnership can be said to have provided a well-intentioned, but rather hazy, sense of direction and purpose.

The view taken here, is that partnership principles are probably coming to the end of their natural shelf life. They have, however, served useful purposes. Firstly, they have provided a focal point for a growing number of people (both professionals and parents) who are committed to a view of education in which families and schools work *together*, as part of a shared enterprise for their mutual benefit, and especially for the benefit of pupils. Secondly, they have provided an important antidote to the prevailing market view of education, in which parents have been given a minor, supporting role in their children's schooling.

At this stage of the evolution of home–school work, however, continuing overuse of the term 'partnership' is tending to prevent more serious consideration of:

- the continuing gaps between the rhetoric and actual achievement — partnership is very easy to talk about, very hard to achieve;
- the intellectual limitations of partnership ideals and their relevance to the real world;
- the development of alternative and complementary strategies, that are required to open up educational opportunities to *all* pupils and their families.

No matter how well families and schools can learn to work together, there will always be a need to complement such practical partnerships, with specific provision for professional and parental needs respectively. For parents, this might include the provision of independent information, advice and support; it might include the availability of people with specialist knowledge, skill and experience through advocacy schemes: finally it would tap, (through 'mentoring' schemes) the increased familiarity and confidence that some parents acquire through their contact with, and involvement in, their children's schools.

### A School's Work with Parents: Key Features on the Landscape

Previous sections have described a range of powerful, sometimes contradictory, influences on the development of a school's work with parents. In this section, an attempt is made to profile some of the elements of mainstream practice which are likely to impinge most on the working lives of schools and teachers everywhere.

In a very real sense, government legislation will have widely differing effects on schools and families, according to their type, situation and circumstances. So, for example, legal requirements will impact differently on early years, primary and secondary provision; inner city schools, with multilingual populations or bilingual majorities, present different challenges and opportunities to those presented by rural schools with scattered populations; finally, special schools, too, have their own, widely differing strengths, needs and circumstances. Taken together, then, the profile of any school's activities is likely to be seen as a mixture of general demands and opportunities, which are system-wide, and a special dimension which consists of an institution's response to its own situation, structural features, previous experience, even acknowledging the contribution of individual personalities.

Firstly, in general terms, headteachers, senior managers and those with pastoral responsibilities are likely to have more contact with parents than classroom teachers, particularly where that contact is rooted in work and behaviour problems that demand wider attention. Because home–school liaison teachers are the only staff members, apart from the senior management team, to have direct contact with parents, families and a range of agencies who work with them, this can create tensions of different kinds. Liaison, by definition, involves mediation. Many home–school liaison teachers describe this as a situation in which the bullets come from all directions!

Secondly, it is self-evident that teachers of younger children (and those who work with them, such as nursery nurses, bilingual classroom assistants etc.) have more informal, daily contact with parents and carers, than teachers of older pupils. This is one of many ways in which primary and secondary schools are very different places, both to work in and visit.

Thirdly, although the range, variety and frequency of contacts between families and schools have generally increased, it remains true that much teacher/parent contact is limited, one way — and on the school's terms. The combined effects of government requirement and professional response don't seem to have made a great deal of difference here. Relatively few teachers have regular, sustained or in-depth contact with the parents/carers of the children that they teach. This helps to explain the continuing concern of many schools (and of those involved in home–school liaison in particular) to raise the profile of work with parents/carers, in order both to improve the quality of existing contacts and to broaden the base of both school initiatives and parental response.

The immediate and obvious effects of the legislation concerning parental 'choice', or rather 'preference', of schools, have been the subject of political hype and unsubstantiated claim. There are, however, several significant patterns.

The general impact of this legislation has had a cumulative effect on (mainly secondary) schools and a sharp impact upon a few. The cumulative effect of this has been steadily to polarize schools on the grounds of social differences (where geography, transport etc. make this possible), and to sharply polarize a number of inner city schools on the combined grounds of race and pupil achievement. This has served to make many inner city multicultural schools, doing a good job in challenging circumstances, vulnerable to negative parent grapevines and damaging, though shallow, reports following a formal inspection. OFSTED inspections, in general, and the prior meeting of parents in particular, seems to engender fear, panic, even hysteria on a grand scale. This is a temporary state which usually disappears with the source of the cause!

Negative reactions in this area include the instant introduction and brushing up of policies, the use of meaningless statistics to show how healthy parent participation and involvement is, and attempts to 'engineer' an uncritical group of parents for the registered inspector running the discussion. Such evidence as there is suggests that schools that are genuinely trying to improve the quality of their work with parents and become more responsive to them have nothing to fear. Registered inspectors are tending to interpret the various agendas set by 'A Framework for Inspection' in a reasonably liberal way. And any group of generally satisfied (but not uncritical!) parents is a huge asset and make good ambassadors for any school. In the event, the inspector's written comments on the quality of home–school work will tend to be both brief and bland in the current scheme of things.

More positively, however, an impending OFSTED inspection can sometimes serve as a catalyst for a genuine review of the strengths and weaknesses of a school's current efforts in this area. This is particularly likely when a critical self review is matched by a genuine attempt to tap into the expectations and experience of parents as a whole. This kind of 'home–school audit', incidentally, is probably the best starting point for the development of effective policy.

Probably the biggest impact of both government legislation and concerning parents and real life carers is in the field of 'reporting pupil achievement'. Here the combined demands of the production of regular reports based on a variety of forms of assessment and recording, combined with the arrangements for teachers and parents, (and, increasingly, pupils and teachers), to review the progress of individual pupils and to set future targets, give this work high profile in the working lives of teachers, and make parents a more tangible presence. On the other hand, the requirements to provide essential, basic information about the life and work of the school for new and prospective parents and regular information about the curriculum, children's programmes of work etc., whilst part of the school's legal obligations, do not impinge greatly upon the lives of many of its teachers.

The other major impact of the combined effects of government policy and resource allocation, has been the steadily increasing pressure on schools to provide, through sponsorship and more established forms of fundraising, a substantial proportion of their running costs, particularly in small primary schools. Recent studies (Mountfield, 1991; NCPTA, 1994) estimate this largely parent donated subsidy at around 200 million pounds per year. In a few areas, where this is politically acceptable, this funding has even started to include the funding of particular teaching posts and additional members of staff.

*Table 9.2: The official view*

---

Parents should ensure that their children arrive at school on time; that their appearance is reasonable, clean and tidy; that they have had some breakfast. Most do already. Alas, some do not.
**John Patten**, Guardian 6/3/1993

I believe we do share in the objective of raising standards and we would welcome your help in encouraging parents to be more aware of their role as challenging yet supportive partners in education.
**Baroness Blatch**, NCPTA Conference Birmingham '94 (DfE News. 102/1994)

Schools should make every effort to encourage parents to acknowledge their own importance in helping their children.
**DfE**, Pupil Behaviour and Discipline Circ. 8/1994

Your knowledge, views and experience as a parent are vital in helping your child to develop. Your child is likely to make most progress if you, your child's school and the LEA all work in partnership.

**You as a parent, have a right to take part in decisions about your child's education and to be kept in touch at all stages. Your views and support are very important**.
Special Educational Needs: A Guide for Parents (DfE, 1994)

Children's progress will be diminished if their parents are not seen as partners in the educational process with unique knowledge and information to impart. Professional help can seldom be wholly effective unless it builds upon parents' capacity to be involved and unless parents consider that professionals take account of what they say and treat their views and anxieties as intrinsically important.
Special Educational Needs: Code of Practice 1994

---

These practical developments, which are the outcomes of the Government's political ideology and its approach to the work of (state) schools, serve to reinforce the presence of parents and their rights as consumers. They also define a significant and more developed role for them in their children's schooling. By their very nature they also have implications for the work of all schools and all teachers. There is also some evidence, based on speeches and publications, that the official view of these relationships is, itself, changing in positive ways, as accompanying extracts from official speeches and documents bear witness (see Table 9.2).

Whilst this section has selected those issues and requirements that serve to raise the profile of parents most, there are others. In particular the role and presence of governors and parent governors (and governors in general) can vary enormously from one school to another, but can be substantial. Similarly, the Government's determination to require schools to regularly vote to stay in/ opt out of LEA control will have a differential impact on schools. Up to now, however, what has been noticeable has been the very crude divisions within both teacher and parent opinion that have characterized much of the voting in the past. Finally, a rapidly growing number of schools are involving parents (through consultation or direct involvement) in the formulation of school policies in areas where this is a formal requirement, or where it makes sense to do so.

**Key Tasks**
* Establish clear goals, policies and priorities
* Monitor, review and evaluate the existing programme
* Find ways of bringing together the different views and experience of parents, pupils and teachers
* Facilitate and support appropriate innovation and development, in line with the school's changing aims and the changing expectations of parents
* Identify, and respond to, special needs and circumstances — of individuals and groups

*Source*: *'Working with Parents': A Whole School Approach*, Bastiani, J. (1989)

Such areas, e.g., special educational needs, pupil behaviour/anti-bullying, homework and equal opportunities policies have the same relevance for the parents of younger, as well as older, pupils. Such evidence as there is suggests that such an approach is more satisfying to all those involved, generates a greater sense of commitment and 'ownership', which in turn makes the policies more action-oriented and, therefore, more likely to be effective.

## Towards a 'Whole-school'/Cross-curricular Approach

A school's work with its parents is now a key organizational task for *all* schools and *all* teachers. It is a major concern which is circumscribed by legal requirements and a part of all school development plans. It therefore has to be part of a school's collective planning and corporate efforts; it calls for coordination and consistency, which can only be achieved through a 'whole-school' approach and policy linked effort. Home–school work also provides a periodic focus for planning efforts in key cross-curricular areas, which call for the informed and active interest, support and participation of parents and families. These include assessment, recording and reporting, reading and language development and pastoral care.

In this section, an attempt is made to set an agenda for working with parents, which has a 'feel' for contemporary conditions and recognizes the value and achievements of 'good practice' in this area. It would have application to a wide range of settings and circumstances and, above all, be based upon principled action, which recognizes the key role of parents and families in their children's education and development.

What is needed is a framework for the management, support and fuller development of home–school work which:

* identifies clear and constructive strategies for those who have responsibility for home–school work, in senior management teams and pastoral structures (see Table 9.3).
* embeds 'good practice' in the work of *all* schools and *all* teachers.
* incorporates the particular knowledge, skill and experience of those who have specialist home–school liaison expertise.

*John Bastiani*

Table 9.4:  *Home–school audit: The basic ingredients*

---

- Mission statements
- Current legal requirements: LEA policies and initiatives
- Review of existing provision
- Portrayal of parental expectations and experience
- Other views and perspectives

---

### Doing a Home–School Audit: Developing a Policy

One of the most effective ways in which schools, of all sizes and types, can improve their work with parents is to carry out a home–school audit, from which a policy is developed. For this provides an excellent focus for a collective look at what the school has set out to do, what it has achieved and what it should attempt to do next.

A home–school audit provides a sufficiently broad and flexible framework (see Table 9.4) to accommodate the wide-ranging requirements that now characterize home–school work; it can readily accommodate the diverse and differing views of school staff, parents, governors, (and, where appropriate, pupils too). Above all it gives emphasis to a review of existing practice, which is rooted in the collection of information and evidence, rather than wishful thinking or beguiling rhetoric. Finally, it calls for the formulation of a clear policy, achieved through discussion, which spells out what the next steps are, how they are to be achieved, and by whom. Such a process, too, if it is genuinely consultative and self-critical, actually helps to strengthen the very processes of cooperation and partnership that it seeks to endorse. There are now a growing number of practical instruments and activities for carrying out such a task, together with suggestions for their use and further development (see Alexander *et al.*, 1995).

A home–school audit is a way of focusing a school's collective energy on a key aspect of its work, in a concentrated, and effective way. It helps to identify strengths and weaknesses, suggest priorities and point the way to planned improvements. There is also a rapidly growing number of schools, of all kinds, who are themselves producing both general home–school policies and other areas which call for some consideration of the contribution of parents (e.g., homework, pupil behaviour, equal opportunities and a range of curriculum related topics.) These provide a valuable source of reference and comparison with one's own efforts.

### 'Mainstreaming' Good Ideas and Effective Practice

'Mainstreaming' home–school work seems to give it a higher profile and greater status in the life and work of the school as a whole. It can do this through a range of strategies. These might include the organization of staff time and responsibilities, such as the allocation of responsibility for individuals to work with parents and the use of INSET and professional development.

Above all, a school can seek to embed developing good practice by making sure that this work is very definitely 'on the agenda', for all staff, and both part of the routines and normal functioning of the school as a whole, as well as having its own characteristic slots and efforts. There are a great many, very different opportunities for doing this. They include:

- arrangements for new parents (information, meetings, home visits);
- reporting pupil achievement (written reports: teacher/parent consultations etc.);
- parent newsletters;
- curriculum sessions for parents;
- special meetings for parents (e.g., 'pre-OFSTED' inspection: annual governors report);
- developing a whole school policy for working with parents;
- staff meetings (whole staff, senior management, pastoral work with tutors/class teachers); and
- staff training: INSET.

### INSET and Professional Development

Opportunities for teachers to prepare to work with parents and families during training, and to consolidate and develop the capacity to do this work more effectively 'on the job' are, at best, minimal and unsystematic, and at worst, non-existent (see Atkin and Bastiani, 1984). This remains true in spite of the current emphasis on school-based and practice-linked initial training. At the moment there is a clear recognition that both initial and post experience training and development opportunities are sorely needed: on the other hand, there is little consensus about what should be done, by whom and when.

Following the arguments and evidence produced here, what is clearly needed is an approach which contains:

- national guidelines and initatives; the piloting of ideas; the networking of 'good practice' (at both initial and post-experience levels). This should be established by consultation with all the main parties involved, (parent organizations as well as professional bodies).
- elements of initial training for all teachers which help prepare teachers to work more effectively with parents, carers and families (not just a few optional odds and sods in 'early years' and 'special needs' modules.) This should genuinely reflect the current concerns and considerable achievements of home–school work in Britain now, not be stuck in a time warp. It should also include induction and mentoring schemes for newly qualified and recently appointed staff.

Table 9.5:  *Some training/INSET themes and topics*

---

**A   For ALL teachers**
- practical communication with parents (IT and INSET);
- reporting pupil achievement;
- involving parents and teachers more effectively in the life and work of the school;
- running curriculum workshops; and
- how parents can help. . .

**B   For teachers with special interest in, responsibility for, home–school work**
- working with families;
- running parents' groups;
- making the most of home visits; and
- working with other agencies.

**C   Management training and development**
- developing a whole-school approach: developing a home–school policy;
- doing a home–school audit;
- involving parents in management/policy making; and
- mainstreaming good ideas and effective practice.

---

- a framework and core of materials and activities to support school-based professional development. These should cover and go beyond the basic legal requirements to extend the work of teachers and also provide some opportunities for joint training, the involvement of parents where appropriate etc.
- a wider programme of INSET and professional development activities, regionally based, to act as a catalyst and provide support for, both a wider and developing view of parents, which both on occasions challenges prevailing assumptions and provides positive encouragement and practical support. Much of this training and development work can, and should be, intensely practical. It should also be linked to a more realistic approach to what teachers are actually required to do (see Table 9.5).

By any standard, home–school work in Britain has contributed a great deal and has much to celebrate. Often pursued from a deep commitment and a proselytizing style, it has developed a wide-ranging and effective repertoire of good practice. Much of this has been within a model of education which stresses the broad purposes of education, egalitarian ideologies and an extension of teacher roles. It has achieved a great deal — for pupils, families and schools alike — often for many of those children and families who have got little out of the education system so far.

In recent years, however, political interest, the accumulation of research evidence and professional experience and the growing expectations and active interest of parents as a whole, have combined to create a very broad interest in parental rights and obligations and in their role as co-educators of their children. As a result of this important and far-reaching change of scope and emphasis, the importance of working effectively with parents has now become a major task for *all* schools and *all* teachers. This applies to everyone, regardless of the extent and type of their previous experience, or the differences of contact and circumstance within which they currently work.

This chapter has outlined something of both the case and direction for a whole school approach, which combines a need to develop effective strategies for working with parents of children of different ages and capabilities. It is linked across the main areas of curriculum and organization and anchored into the broader aspects of the life and work of the school. At the same time, schools need to recognize and learn from the most important lessons of home–school liaison, adapting them to their own needs and circumstances. To be genuine and have a lasting impact, such developments will need to incorporate a growing willingness to consult, involve and listen to, the many voices of parents themselves. There is some scope here for cautious and qualified optimism. In areas where this is happening, in the development of more responsive reporting, in shared policy making, in joint teacher/parent activity and combined effort, the results are often immediately impressive and have substantial effects. And nothing succeeds like success!

## References

ALEXANDER, T., BASTIANI, J. and BERESFORD, E. (1995) *Home–School Policies: A Practical Guide*, Nottingham, JET Publications.

ATKIN, J. and BASTIANI, J. (1984) *Preparing Teachers to Work with Parents: A Survey of Initial Training*, Nottingham, University of Nottingham School of Education.

BASTIANI, J. (1989) *Parents and Teachers (3), Working with Parents: A Whole School Approach*, London, Routledge.

BASTIANI, J. (1993) *UK Directory of Home–School Initiatives*, (2nd ed.), London, RSA.

BASTIANI, J. and DOYLE, N. (1994) *Home and School: Building a Better Partnership*, London, National Consumer Council.

DES (1991) *Parent's Charter: You and Your Child's Education*, London, DES.

DfE (1994) *Parent's Charter: Our Children's Education, the Updated Parent's Charter*, London, DfE.

GOLDSTEIN, H. (1991) *Assessment in Schools*, London, IPPR.

MACBETH, A. (1989) *Involving Parents*, London, Heinemann.

MANSFIELD, M. (1994) *Practice Makes Perfect*, London, Campaign For State Education.

MORTIMORE, P., SAMMONS, P., STOLL, L., LEWIS, D. and ECOL, R. (1988) *School Matters: The Junior Years*, Wells, Open Books.

MOUNTFIELD, A. (1991) *State Schools: A Suitable Case for Charity*, London, Directory of Social Change publications.

MUNN, P. (Ed) (1993) *Parents and Schools: Customers, Managers or Partners*, London, Routledge.

NCPTA (1994) *The State of Our Schools: A Follow up Survey*, London, NCPTA.

WOLFENDALE, S. (1993) *Empowering Parents and Teachers: For Children*, London, Cassell.

Chapter 10

# Leading Cross-curricular Practice

*Rosemary Webb and Graham Vulliamy*

This chapter provides advice on how to coordinate and develop cross-curricular practice in the areas covered in the preceeding chapters. However, it will also be relevant to initiating review and development work in relation to other cross-curricular dimensions, skills and themes. It considers how initiatives may be set in motion both within the classrooms of individual teachers and in classrooms across the school as part of a whole-school approach to change.

## The Nature of Cross-curricular Practice

The fact that cross-curricular practice is non-statutory, combined with the pressure on curriculum time of National Curriculum knowledge requirements, the importance attributed to the basics of numeracy and literacy (see, for example, Dearing, 1993 and OFSTED, 1995) and the possible impact on the curriculum of national testing in the core subjects at ages 7 and 11 years, means that cross-curricular practice tends to be under-represented in whole school planning and policies. For example, in her research into the implementation of the National Curriculum at Key Stage 2, Webb (1993) reported that with the exception of a few schools the themes identified by the National Curriculum Council (NCC, 1990) were not being incorporated into schools' plans apart from information in some areas, such as health education, which were already well-established and frequently incorporated into topic work. The heavy work demands currently expected of classteachers as a result of the Education Reform Act (1988) and subsequent legislation make it very difficult for them to find the time and energy to plan for, and to introduce, new initiatives. However, even in the context of the original grossly overloaded National Curriculum some teachers were still determined to continue to develop the cross-curricular practice that they valued (Vulliamy and Webb, 1993) and to make space for additional material that they considered particularly relevant and motivating for pupils (Webb, 1993).

Increased opportunities for schools to develop the curriculum according to their own preferences are provided by the post-Dearing reductions to National Curriculum content and the notion of covering the programmes of study either in depth or in outline proposed by SCAA at their regional conferences to disseminate findings on the consultation over the new Orders. These give encouragement for individual teachers and schools who want to develop new interests and expertise and to shape the curriculum to take particular account of their pupils and the local community. Our current research into curriculum change in six schools, as part of an English-Finnish comparative project, certainly suggests that, while devising new long- and medium-term plans in accordance with the requirements of the new Orders, schools are taking the opportunity to rethink their aims and values and to ensure that these, as well as national priorities and directives, determine the nature and content of their teaching. If the promised five year moratorium on curriculum change is sustained, then as teachers grow in familiarity and confidence in teaching the National Curriculum they are likely to identify more cross-curricular possibilities and wish to experiment.

Traditionally primary schools have adopted a form of curriculum organization which integrates aspects of subjects within topics. Consequently, primary teachers have a wealth of experience to draw on in planning and teaching cross-curricular themes. Since the introduction of the National Curriculum, especially at Key Stage 2, schools have been moving away from broad-based topics encompassing a range of subjects towards more subject-focused topics which only draw on material from two or three subjects (see, for example, Webb and Vulliamy, 1996). This move has been both to meet more readily the subject requirements of the National Curriculum and in response to the steadily mounting criticisms of topic work for fostering artificial links between the subject components, giving rise to aimless copying from books, providing pupils with a very superficial experience of subjects and negligible opportunities for progression (see, for example, Alexander *et al.*, 1992). However, as demonstrated by Woods (1993), topic work has immense possibilities for pupil motivation and learning and teacher creativity and professional development. His study of critical events in teaching and learning, which are of the same genre as topics, included: primary children writing a noted children's book (Rushavenn Time); the making of a film of a village community (Laxfield, Suffolk); the design of a heritage centre in Winchester; and an archaeological project on a Romano-British site in south London. In our research an example of a topic with a cross-curricular theme as its main focus was carried out over half a term by the two classes in a small school. The children designed a nature trail using the environment around the village and when it was completed invited the children from a city school, with whom they corresponded, to come and experience and evaluate it.

In addition to being the focus of a topic, cross-curricular themes can be incorporated into the curriculum in a variety of other ways:

- as continuing work (for example, a series of KS1 assemblies or timetabled Year 6 discussion sessions might be devoted to aspects of citizenship);
- taught through subject lessons and topics (for example, media education

might be developed through the production of a class newspaper as
an English activity or as part of a topic based on a visit to France); and

- as a distinct block of work for one or two days or each afternoon for
a week (for example, work in health education on the use and misuse
of substances such as alcohol).

Cross-curricular skills — such as learning English as a second language,
pupil self-assessment, problem solving, study skills and the skills of observation — are developed in different contexts across the whole curriculum. There
are an enormous number of such skills and potential ways in which they can
be grouped for the purposes of planning, monitoring and assessing pupil
progress. Consequently, schools identify for particular attention those that they
consider especially important for their pupils. In planning for consistency and
coherence in the teaching of these skills schools are concerned:

- to establish progression;
- to identify the ways in which attainment in one set of skills influences
progress in particular subjects — for example, communication skills
are important in many aspects of technology;
- to recognize which skills are independent of curriculum content and
readily transferable and which vary in their usage according to subject
context — for example, different aspects of observational skills are
emphasized according to whether they are being used to analyse a
historic artefact, paint a flower in art or record what happens in a
science experiment.

Through the whole curriculum, teaching methods, staff–pupil relationships, resources and the overall ethos to which these contribute, schools aim
to provide equality of opportunity for all pupils by meeting their diverse needs
and helping them to maximize their abilities and interests. The cross-curricular
dimensions are enormously important in enabling this to happen through
fostering policies and practices which counter discrimination, stereotypes and
prejudices and remove both the obvious and the more subtle barriers to children's achievement and enjoyment of school. In this book work with parents
and meeting special educational needs in the classroom are singled out for
attention. The growing literature of research and advice on these two areas is
a testament to their importance. Two other vital dimensions for which much
assistance is already available are multi-cultural and anti-racist education and
equal opportunities in relation to gender and anti-sexist initiatives (see, for
example, Tutchell, 1990; Claire *et al.*, 1993; Verma and Pumfrey, 1994).

## The Role of Coordinators

Depending on their values, training and experiences many primary teachers
regard particular aspects of cross-curricular practice as very important.

Consequently, these may be emphasized within their teaching. Also, it is often the case in relation to cross-curricular practice that the expertise and conviction of individual teachers leads them to generate interest among their colleagues and to provide leadership voluntarily. However, increasingly teachers are being asked by the head or senior management team to assume coordinating responsibilities for particular cross-curricular dimensions, skills or themes. This is likely to occur in preparation for, or as a consequence of, an OFSTED inspection owing to the importance attached by OFSTED to reviewing pupils' spiritual, moral, cultural and social development as part of their inspection schedule (OFSTED, 1994). In some schools this has led to consideration of the ways in which the school ethos, community and curriculum provide opportunities for pupils to extend their personal experience in these areas. Aspects of cross-curricular practice may be regarded as a subset of, or closely related to, existing responsibilities — for example English coordinators could decide to use their subject as a vehicle to explore the possibilities of media education. However, frequently, new responsibilities in cross-curricular practice are likely to be allocated to teachers in addition to coordination of one or more National Curriculum subjects. As discussed in Chapter 1, the introduction of the Code of Practice on the Identification and Assessment of Special Educational Needs (1994) has led those schools, which did not have a teacher with responsibility for special educational needs, to appoint a Special Educational Needs Coordinator (SENCO).

While acknowledging that, because it is often of low profile and status, coordinating cross-curricular practice is generally a different enterprise from coordinating National Curriculum subjects, it is still useful to consider briefly what can be learned from the latter. Based on our qualitative research into the changing roles and responsibilities of primary teachers, which was conducted in fifty primary schools across thirteen LEAs, Webb and Vulliamy (1996) discuss how the demands of the National Curriculum and its assessment procedures have legitimated and expanded the role of curriculum coordinators. We suggest that curriculum coordinators are playing a major role in curriculum planning and policy-making and raising the collective confidence of staff in their subjects. We identify the following ways in which curriculum coordinators are contributing to the organization and development of their subject:

- overseeing resources and controlling subject budgets;
- advising on teaching materials;
- familiarizing colleagues with the subject Orders;
- attending courses and feeding back information;
- contributing to plans;
- developing policy documents;
- providing information for parents and governors;
- liaising with other schools;
- organizing or providing INSET;

- working alongside colleagues in the classroom to develop practice; and
- monitoring subject implementation.

The last three aspects of the role were viewed as particularly demanding for coordinators and requiring both considerable inter-personal skills and new professional skills not traditionally associated with primary teaching, such as those needed to support adult learning and to carry out classroom observations. The main factors which coordinators considered facilitated their work were support of the headteacher, the provision of non-contact time and a school culture in which teachers were prepared to be guided by, and to work cooperatively, with their colleagues. Conversely, the lack of these factors were identified as major constraints. Most teachers were coordinators for at least one subject. However, depending on the availability of responsibility points linked to pay incentives, coordinators were differentially rewarded in terms of status and salary enhancement for what was often essentially the same work.

In Chapter 6 Joy Palmer emphasizes the need for leadership and coordination to be provided in environmental education and suggests ways in which this might be achieved. Adapting her suggestions to take account of the range of cross-curricular practice represented in this book gives rise to the following patterns:

- each teacher agrees to take responsibility for incorporating specified aspects of cross-curricular practice in his/her teaching;
- a coordinator of a curriculum subject or area of school life incorporates an aspect of cross-curricular practice into his/her responsibilities — for example, discipline might be incorporated within pastoral responsibilities;
- an individual coordinator or a team coordinates related aspects, such as inter-related cross-curricular themes; and
- an individual coordinator or a team coordinates an aspect of cross-curricular practice, such as work with parents.

## Taking the Lead

All primary teachers have a vital management function within the classroom and the majority have school wide management roles. Increasingly beginning teachers are also expected to assume some whole school responsibilities. However, in connection with the promotion and development of cross-curricular practice, because of its lack of status, financial remuneration and often voluntary nature, proponents are more likely to be concerned with aspects of leadership rather than management. While managers are expected to lead, leaders may not always be able to create opportunities to manage. Whitaker (1993) points out that it is important to appreciate the essential difference between management and leadership functions. On the one hand, he considers management to be concerned with:

- orderly structures;
- maintaining day-to-day functions;
- ensuring that work gets done;
- monitoring outcomes and results; and
- efficiency. (p.74)

On the other hand, he describes leadership as being concerned with:

- personal and interpersonal behaviour;
- focus on the future;
- change and development;
- quality; and
- effectiveness. (p.74)

Teachers in a senior management role are likely to find it easier to generate interest in, and to promote, cross-curricular work among colleagues because of their additional status and power to make things happen. However, increasingly in education it is recognized that, if schools are to develop and improve, the skills and abilities of all staff must be harnessed and ways found to encourage and to empower everyone to take a full and active leadership role. All teachers, including beginning teachers and part-time teachers, can take the lead in raising staff awareness of issues in cross-curricular practice and initiating review and development.

Webb (1994) found that young teachers often lacked experience of sharing their classroom practice with colleagues and were concerned particularly about trying to influence the practice of older and more senior members of staff. As one young subject coordinator put it:

> Personally I find it quite hard sometimes because I'm very aware that a lot of members of staff have got a great deal of expertise and experience, whereas I am very new. I think they can offer a great deal to me. I'm very aware of drawing on them. (p.67)

Harrison (1996) acknowledges that new entrants to teaching are very likely to feel that they have little to offer to experienced teachers. However, he rightly reassures them that this is not the case because their initial training will possibly make them more familiar with up-to-date subject content and teaching approaches than their colleagues and the discussions that they have had in seminars and tutorials will prepare them for presenting information and arguments to colleagues. Also, and most importantly for cross-curricular practice:

> The fact that you have recently been in as many as four different schools, examined their teaching and learning policies, have seen

teachers' many different methods of organizing their classrooms, witnessed whole-school discipline practices and the ways in which children's special needs were met or the ways text-books are used [means] you do have a contribution to make. (Harrison, 1996, p.3)

Given the importance of the head's support, if beginning teachers wish their work to have an impact beyond their own classroom then clearly it will be vital to discuss commitment to an area with him or her and to explore possible avenues for development. Prior to such a discussion, it will be helpful to have considered how this might relate to other school initiatives and to those priorities within the school development plan and to have mapped out in advance an outline of the ideal action-plan. Given the scarcity of non-contact time, unless the area is viewed as a school priority as is currently the case with SEN in many schools, then ideas of what might be accomplished will have to be within the limits of whatever is feasible in time after school.

There are different approaches to leadership and the most effective leaders take stock of the school context, the nature of the initiative that they wish to promote, the personalities involved and adopt a style and devise strategies to fit that situation. Four broad approaches to promoting cross-curricular practice are:

- leading by example (stimulating interest among colleagues and demonstrating the possibilities of the area of interest through personal practice and taking opportunities to publicize it through displays, 'good work' assemblies, contributions to school publications and concerts);
- collaborating (building relationships, drawing on others' experience and generating interest and commitment among one or more colleagues to undertake a small-scale joint project);
- supporting (providing ideas and resources, answering queries, solving difficulties and acknowledging and praising quality work); and
- delegating (encouraging others to assume responsibilities for tasks and to participate in initiatives in ways that develop their confidence, knowledge and aptitudes).

Each of these strategies might be used in isolation initially, but once staff interest is aroused it is more likely that two or more will be in operation simultaneously. In order to introduce an area of work which is new, such as media education, leading by example may be the best, or perhaps the only, way to begin. Also, the provision of ideas and resources for class activities can be a good starting point. Once staff have become motivated to try out some of these and begin to devise ideas for themselves, it may be possible to set up a joint project. In areas where there is already staff recognition that work needs to be done, such as currently exists in several schools in relation to discipline and the teaching of English as a second language, it may be possible to form a team immediately to begin some development work. In areas, such as SEN, where legislative requirements have implications for all teachers, the participation of staff may quickly lead to all four strategies becoming appropriate.

### Acting on Information Gathered

In Chapter 2 Pamela Munn demonstrates how building up a picture of classroom interaction and the implications of actions taken can assist teachers in identifying ways of improving their practice. She emphasizes the value of teachers sharing accounts of how they manage discipline in their classrooms and reflecting on these together in order to identify ways forward. Sharing classroom experiences is an important way in which student teachers and beginning teachers get access to the knowledge of classroom management of experienced teachers. Reflecting on and analysing practice in pairs or small groups also provides a valuable source of professional development for all teachers. Day *et al.* (1993) use the term 'critical friends' to refer to such practical partnerships between equals, which can be forged to exchange understandings, overcome difficulties and act as a catalyst for ideas. In advice on getting started in working in this way, they suggest formalizing the partnership, viewing it as helpful to establish some ground rules — perhaps even draw up a written contract — to clarify mutual expectations of the major goals to be pursued and the processes involved. Agreeing on the processes involved is vitally important because professional comments on sensitive or problematic issues can readily be taken for personal criticism.

Having a specific focus and outcome for the partnership and a timescale in which it might be achieved provides structure to the work. As observed by NCC (1990), cross-curricular themes, skills and dimensions provide a considerable agenda for the development of classroom practice:

> If the whole curriculum is to mean anything then it must be imparted by use of a wide range of teaching methods, formal and informal, class and group, didactic and practical. The wide range of skills which pupils must acquire must be reflected in an equally wide variety of approaches to teaching. (NCC, 1990, p.7)

Teaching, which includes more democratic and cooperative approaches encouraging pupils to make decisions, exercise judgments and to plan and evaluate their own learning, plays an important part in cross-curricular themes and is central to education for citizenship and global education. Consequently, any of the following questions could provide a starting point for pairs of teachers to review their practice in this respect:

- How do I promote trust among pupils and between them and myself?
- How are conflicts resolved?

- Are pupils encouraged to develop and clarify their own value systems?
- In what ways do pupils actively participate in lessons and how might this be extended — for example, through small group discussion, simulation and role-play?
- What opportunities are provided for cooperative learning and how are these regarded by the pupils?
- How much use do I make of open-ended questions and tasks?
- How far are pupils helped to evalute the processes and outcomes of their learning?

In order to gain further data to inform their reflections 'critical friends' may also observe each other's teaching or share audio or videotapes of lessons. In relation to reporting back on classroom observations Whitaker (1993) has some useful advice. He identifies four key factors to be taken account of in providing feedback:

- be specific and concrete, comment only on what was actually seen and heard;
- be brief, limit feedback to a few key observations;
- be descriptive, provide details of behaviours not interpretations; and
- be reflective, encourage responses which reflect critically on the experience.

He emphasizes the importance of listening and stresses that 'handled badly, feedback will tend to close down rather than stimulate the reflective capacity' (p.129).

In order to obtain a wider view of cross-curricular themes, skills or dimensions across the whole school an audit could be undertaken. This would have the aim of finding out what is happening already and of obtaining participants' views about it and how it might be futher supported. In order to provide an example of the kinds of questions which might be used to structure such an audit, Table 10.1 poses some questions that might be asked in an audit of media education.

In Chapter 6 Joy Palmer recomends an 'environmental audit' as a useful way of assessing the contribution of all areas of school life to environmental education. She suggests that the 'audit' might be carried out guided by key questions focusing on existing documentation, resources, lesson content, pupil perspectives, acknowledgment of achievement and the degree of match between school rhetoric and classroom reality. In the context of developing a policy for working with parents John Bastiani also endorses the value of carrying out an audit to look at the school's intentions and how far these have been met in order to root a review of existing practice in evidence supplied by all participants rather than 'wishful thinking or beguiling rhetoric'.

The introduction of OFSTED inspections into the primary sector has led headteachers and curriculum coordinators to be increasingly concerned to find

- How do teachers define media education and what activities do they view it as including?
- What forms of media education are already offered (using visual, audio, print or computer materials)?
- What books and resources are available in school or can be borrowed from elsewhere?
- How might children's media experiences be incorporated into teaching?
- Which staff/governors/parents have a particular interest and or expertise in aspects of media education?
- How might any forthcoming trips, visitors to the school and involvement in the community contribute to media education?
- Has the LEA a policy and or guidelines containing advice on media education?
- How might the school monitor its work on media education?
- What changes and new ideas need to be introduced into the curriculum and over what timescale?
- How will the success of media education be judged?

ways of gathering evidence in order to monitor practice across the whole school — in the first instance to find out what is happening and in the second to implement steps to improve it. Webb and Vulliamy (1996) list the following ways in which coordinators sought to find out about existing practice in their subject, of which the first four were the most common:

- looking at displays in shared areas and classrooms;
- scrutinizing medium- and short-term plans;
- listening to staffroom conversation;
- 'popping in' to colleagues' classrooms e.g., when working with a student teacher;
- talking to pupils about their work;
- discussions or informal interviews with colleagues; and
- classroom observations.

With the exception of classroom observations, the other approaches to collecting evidence can all be carried out without non-contact time. Gaining pupils' perspectives on issues and initiatives is often an underused source of information for reviews of practice. If the reason behind the questions is fully explained pupils can usually supply illuminative comments on their experiences and often offer practical suggestions for improvements.

Carrying out an 'audit' could become the first stage in an action-research project to develop an aspect of cross-curricular practice. Action research as a means of gaining deeper understanding of a problematic issue and devising ways forward has a long and varied history (see, for example, Webb, 1990) and there is a growing literature demonstrating its value to teachers as a means of developing policy and practice. It has been defined as:

Any systematic inquiry, large or small, conducted by professionals and focusing on some aspect of their practice in order to find out more

Table 10.2: Action research on volunteer helpers in the classroom review

**Review** In the spring term information was collected from volunteer helpers about the kinds of help that they provided, and would like to provide, for their own and other children and the factors which assisted them to be comfortable, confident and effective in the classroom and those which constrained the assistance that they could provide. Classteachers also gave their views and suggestions on these issues.

**Diagnosis**
Analysis of the data collected suggested that volunteer helpers would find it useful:

- to have a guide as to the kinds of help that they might provide, teacher's expectations of them and classroom routines and management; and
- a system of attaching new volunteers to parents who were well established in the school.

**Planning**
A working group of classteachers and parents drafted a guide which was circulated to staff, governors and members of the 'Friends of the School'. This included discussion of the role of parent mentors and three parents agreed to trial the role.

**Implementation**
The guide and mentoring system was put into practice throughout the school at the beginning of the autumn term.

**Monitoring**
Evaluative comments were collected from parents by one of the parent governors in the following February and the classteachers held a meeting where they considered these comments and discussed the advantages and disadvantages of the new system. As a result some amendments were made to the guidance and an evening workshop was provided for all parents who were interested in assisting in the classroom.

about it, and eventually to act in ways they see as better or more effective. (Oberg and McCutcheon, 1989, p.117)

However, many definitions of action research incorporate the notion of a cycle or spiral which involves identifying a problem, devising and implementing a proposed solution and researching the effects of this:

> this total process — review, diagnosis, planning, implementation, monitoring effects — is called action research, and it provides the necessary link between self-evaluation and professional development. (Elliott, 1981, p.ii)

As an illustration of the practical contribution of action research and the stages in the process Table 10.2 provides a description of a project focussing on volunteer helpers in the classroom. This was initiated by the head and two teachers in an infant school as an aspect of the dimension of working with parents.

Plentiful advice exists on designing a project and formulating research questions (see, for example, Vulliamy and Webb, 1992a) and selecting the most appropriate techniques for data collection (see, for example, McKernan,

1991; Altrichter *et al.*, 1993). Action-research evidence can be gathered through a range of data collection techniques including:

- interviews (Powney and Watts, 1987);
- observations (Wragg, 1994);
- diaries (Holly, 1984); and
- document analysis (Hitchcock and Hughes, 1989, Ch.5).

In relation to data collection from pupils, strategies can be devised to give additional access to their views, such as group discussions, simulations, and pupil diaries and drawings.

The evidence thus collected is used to question prior assumptions and to challenge existing beliefs and established practices. Consequently, action research is always a form of self-reflective enquiry and for this reason can in the early stages often be an uncomfortable, even threatening, process. Researching with a 'critical friend' or as a member of a small group provides moral support on such occasions and helps to keep the momentum of the work going when individuals experience pressure of other commitments or enthusiasm and ideas wane temporarily. Despite difficulties encountered the research process is generally acknowledged to be well worthwhile because solutions to problems are rooted in the views and experiences of the school community and are implemented as hypotheses to be tested out in practice and refined and improved through evaluation. A study of the impact on teachers of carrying out research in the context of the part-time, research-based MA run by the University of York reveals the kinds of contributions that carrying out practitioner research can make to teachers' personal and professional development (Vulliamy and Webb, 1991; 1992b; 1994). They included an increase in self-confidence, the skills of collecting evidence and using it as a basis for decision-making, a deeper understanding of pupils' perspectives on the teaching–learning process derived from collecting pupil data and the ability to take forward initiatives in the areas on which projects focussed.

Action research may be undertaken by individuals — for example, a teacher might seek to examine her use of praise and censure in her interactions with her own class in order to develop additional strategies to promote good behaviour and to boost pupil self-esteem. However, action research is frequently a collaborative enterprise. For example, in Bradford the LEA have set up a DfE funded Attainment in Multilingual Schools (AIMS) project which is supporting groups of teachers from the LEA's first, middle and high schools in action research into aspects of improving access to the curriculum and the English language skills of their bilingual pupils. Such collaborative enquiry provides a support network for the teachers involved and enables the issues to be investigated from a variety of perspectives and across different subject areas and staff hierarchies. Also, the greater the number of staff involved, the stronger the likely impact of the project and the greater commitment to resultant changes within the schools.

## Disseminating Information and Providing INSET

If the results of a curriculum audit are to be acted on by all staff and/or colleagues are to be informed of initial findings of action research or encouraged to become involved, then it will be important to make sure that all staff are well-informed and kept up-to-date. If possible, this should be done through a staff meeting in order to gauge reactions and allow staff to express their opinions. However, meeting time is precious because there are always plenty of items that could usefully be the focus of the agenda and so maximum use must be made of any opportunity. Webb and Vulliamy (1996) found that the following aspects of organizing meetings were regarded by curriculum co-ordinators as important for successful meetings:

- consideration of the likely effect on colleagues of the timing, duration and venue;
- the preparation of an agenda in consultation with colleagues;
- documentation to inform the meeting which is circulated in advance;
- the taking of minutes, especially notes of points for action;
- keeping to the intended focus of the meeting;
- ways of arriving at shared perceptions and/or agreements on ways forward; and
- deciding when it would be appropriate to include teaching auxillaries, supply teachers, governors, parents.

If it is not possible to share progress or findings directly with staff, then an update could be provided in the form of a sheet of A4 clearly stating the main points, the next steps and any assistance required from colleagues.

In Chapter 9 John Bastiani recognizes the importance of INSET provision to support and inform any whole-school initiative. Depending on school priorities, it may be possible to organize an INSET session in an evening or on a school professional development day. Apart from drawing on findings from a curriculum audit or action research, there are many possibilities for activities which would be interesting, informative and move thinking forward. Webb and Vulliamy (1996) found the activities which curriculum coordinators use as the basis for INSET were many and varied:

- following the advice in commercially produced INSET packs and training videos.
- analysing children's work to identify aspects of quality or the development of skills and concepts.
- listening to a teacher from the school, cluster or a support network presenting ideas and experiences.
- explaining the use of new resources and their implications for practice.
- visiting teachers' classrooms to consider alternative approaches to classroom management.

- watching a video of aspects of classroom practice across the school.
- discussion of successful teaching strategies developed through working alongside colleagues or identified through monitoring.
- sharing findings of paired observation.
- workshops run by LEA advisers or private consultants.
- visiting a school using the resources or equipment that was going to be adopted; and
- whole school attendance at an exhibition or conference. (p.87)

Day *et al.* (1993) suggest that successful INSET activities, whether externally provided or school-based, fulfilled teachers' expectations that they would meet a range of needs:

- Process needs: courses presented a balance of activities, involved working with colleagues, sharing experience, were well-structured.
- Targeting needs: activities were focused upon needs specific to the particular age range taught (i.e., relevant).
- Content needs: courses increased knowledge/awareness, reinforcing and reassuring current thinking but encouraging participants to see issues from different perspectives.
- Utilization needs: courses provided direct curriculum development benefits and application to classroom practice.
- Leadership/modelling needs: activities were led by tutors who were well-prepared, enthusiastic, caring and aware of group dynamics.
- Time and energy needs: courses were timed for when energy levels were high.

Colleagues will provide immediate informal feedback on the success or otherwise of the INSET session through their comments afterwards and the level of interest that they show in involvement in related work in the future. Longer term impact of the INSET can be assessed by whether it features in staff conversations, is reflected in pupil work and whether colleagues request more ideas to try out with their classes. However, in order to make improvements in future INSET activities provided, colleagues could be given a brief open-ended evaluation form on which to make comments and/or asked to supply verbal feedback to three or four key questions.

### Conclusion

While primary school cultures are generally supportive and caring on a personal level, they vary enormously in their ability to foster cooperative endeavour, to facilitate professional development and to be workplaces where staff as well as children can learn together. Fullan and Hargreaves (1992) view such collaborative school cultures as greatly facilitating change and improvement.

Furthermore, they argue that 'In collaborative cultures, teachers develop the collective confidence to respond to change critically, selecting and adapting those elements that will aid improvement in their own work context, and rejecting those that will not' (p.67). Nias *et al.* (1989) provide detailed and fascinating descriptions of five primary schools characterized by positive supportive staff relationships, of which three are viewed as having an all pervasive culture of collaboration. Cultures of collaboration were viewed as being characterized by openness and trust and as valuing equally people as individuals and the groups to which they belong.

Webb and Vulliamy (1996) have described ways in which teachers working together on National Curriculum implementation and assessment have encouraged the sharing of anxieties and ideas and developed collaborative approaches to planning and policymaking. However, we have also noted the growth of more top-down directive managerial styles as a response to the amount and pace of change, the pressures of OFSTED inspections, the adoption of quality assurance mechanisms and increasing accountability to governors and parents. Thus the beliefs and practices associated with collaborative working appear to co-exist in a state of tension with the growth in managerialism. This has meant that much of the collaboration seems to operate at a fairly superficial level. In his research with teachers, Hargreaves (1994) found that the necessity to get together at prescribed times in order to tackle work imposed by external requirements often resulted in what he characterizes as 'contrived collegiality' — 'a safe administrative simulation of collaboration'. 'It replaces spontaneous unpredictable and difficult-to-control forms of teacher generated collaboration with forms of collaboration that are captured, contained and contrived by administrators instead' (p.196).

However, Nias *et al.* (1989) believe teachers have the power to determine the ways in which they work. They argue that:

> Whatever the pressures upon them from outside, primary schools have the capacity to become the kinds of organisations that the adults who work in them choose that they will. Cultures lie within the control of those who participate in them; leaders and members together make their own schools. (Nias *et al.*, 1989, p.186)

Fullan and Hargreaves (1992) agree with this and view it as a responsibility in which everyone should share:

> Educators at all stages of their careers have a responsibility to act — beginning teachers to add new ideas and energies to the profession, and to avoid succumbing to the stale breath of routine; mid-career teachers to get out of the doldrums; and experienced teachers to pass on wisdom instead of cynicism. All have a responsibility to shape the schools of the future so that they are more productive and satisfying places to have a career as a teacher and to be a student. (Fullan and Hargreaves, 1992, p.138)

The reviewing and development of an aspect of cross-curricular practice by a working group or whole school team provides an excellent opportunity for collaboration over an issue selected by them as important rather than one which is allocated because its implementation is mandatory.

## References

ALEXANDER, R., ROSE, J. and WOODHEAD, C. (1992) *Curriculum Organisation and Classroom Practice: A Discussion Paper*, London, DES.

ALTRICHTER, H., POSCH, P. and SOMEKH, B. (1993) *Teachers Investigate Their Work: An Introduction to the Methods of Action Research*, London, Routledge.

CLAIRE, H., MAYBIN, J. and SWANN, J. (Eds) (1993) *Equality Matters: Case Studies from the Primary School*, Clevedon, Multilingual Matters.

DAY, C., HALL, C., GAMMAGE, P. and COLES, M. (1993) *Leadership and Curriculum in the Primary School*, London, Paul Chapman Publishing Ltd.

DEARING, R. (1993) *The National Curriculum and Its Assessment, Final Report*, London, SCAA.

ELLIOTT, J. (1981) *Action-research: A Framework for Self-evaluation in Schools*, TIQL Project, Cambridge, Cambridge Institute of Education.

FULLAN, M. and HARGREAVES, A. (1992) *What's Worth fighting for in Your School*, Buckingham, Open University Press/OPSTF.

HARGREAVES, A. (1994) *Changing Teachers, Changing Times*, London, Cassell.

HARRISON, M. (1996) 'Developing the skills to become an effective Key Stage 2 subject coordinator', in HARRISON, M. (Ed) *Developing a Leadership Role in Key Stage 2 Curriculum*, London, Falmer Press.

HITCHCOCK, G. and HUGHES, D. (1989) *Research and the Teacher: A Qualitative Introduction to School-based Research*, London, Routledge.

HOLLY, M.L. (1984) *Keeping a Personal Professional Journal*, Geelong, Victoria, Deakin University Press.

MCKERNAN, J. (1991) *Curriculum Action Research: A Handbook of Methods and Resources for the Reflective Practitioner*, London, Kogan Page.

NATIONAL CURRICULUM COUNCIL (1990) *The Whole Curriculum, Curriculum Guidance 3*, York, NCC.

NIAS, J., SOUTHWORTH, G. and YEOMANS, R. (1989) *Staff Relationships in the Primary School*, London, Cassell.

OBERG, A. and MCCUTCHEON, G. (1989) 'Teachers' experience doing action research', *Peabody Journal of Education*, **64**, 2, pp.116–27.

OFSTED (1994) *Handbook for the Inspection of Schools*, London, HMSO.

OFSTED (1995) *The Annual Report of Her Majesty's Chief Inspector for Schools, Part 1*, London, HMSO.

POWNEY, J. and WATTS, M. (1987) *Interviewing in Educational Research*, London, Routledge and Kegan Paul.

TUTCHELL, E. (Ed) (1990) *Dolls and Dungarees: Gender Issues in the Primary School Curriculum*, Milton Keynes, Open University Press.

VERMA, G.V. and PUMFREY, P.D. (Eds) (1994) *Cross-curricular Contexts, Themes and Dimensions in the Primary School, Volume 4: Cultural Diversity and the Curriculum*, London, Falmer Press.

VULLIAMY, G. and WEBB, R. (1991) 'Teacher research and educational change: An empirical study', *British Educational Research Journal*, **17**, 3, pp.219–36.

VULLIAMY, G. and WEBB, R. (1992a) 'Designing a teacher-research project', in VULLIAMY, G. and WEBB, R. (Eds) *Teacher Research and Special Educational Needs*, London, David Fulton.

VULLIAMY, G. and WEBB, R. (1992b) 'The influence of teacher research: Process or product?', *Educational Review*, **44**, 1, pp.41–58.

VULLIAMY, G. and WEBB, R. (1993) 'Progressive education and the National Curriculum: Findings from a global education research project', *Educational Review*, **45**, 1, pp.21–41.

VULLIAMY, G. and WEBB, R. (1994) 'Changing classroom practice through teacher research', in CONSTABLE, H., FARROW, S. and NORTON, J. (Eds) *Change in Classroom Practice*, London, Falmer Press.

WEBB, R. (1990) 'The origins and aspirations of practitioner research', in WEBB, R. (Ed) *Practitioner Research in the Primary School*, London, Falmer Press.

WEBB, R. (1993) *Eating the Elephant Bit by Bit: The National Curriculum at Key Stage 2*, London, Association of Teachers and Lecturers.

WEBB, R. (1994) *After the Deluge: Changing Roles and Responsibilities in the Primary School*, London, Association of Teachers and Lecturers.

WEBB, R. and VULLIAMY, G. (1996) *Roles and Responsibilities in the Primary School: Changing Demands, Changing Practices*, Buckingham, Open University Press.

WHITAKER, P. (1993) *Managing Change in Schools*, Buckingham, Open University Press.

WOODS, P. (1993) *Critical Events in Teaching and Learning*, London, Falmer Press.

WRAGG, E.C. (1994) *An Introduction to Classroom Observation*, London, Routledge.

# Notes on Contributors

**John Bastiani** was formerly a tutor in the School of Education at Nottingham University and is now a freelance consultant on home–school matters. He was the Director of RSA's *Parents in a Learning Society* project, is coordinator of the National Home–School Development Group, and has written extensively on the subject of families and schools.

**Margot Brown** has taught in primary schools in Newcastle-upon-Tyne, Inner London, New Zealand and in secondary schools in France. She has worked for Oxfam's Development Education Unit and for the Centre for Urban Educational Studies (ILEA). She is currently national coordinator of the Centre for Global Education at the University College of Ripon and York St John, York.

**Lynne Cameron** is a lecturer in the School of Education, University of Leeds, and has taught at primary and secondary level in Tanzania and the UK. Her research and training interests in first and second language development in education include the learning of English by bilingual pupils, and the in-service training of teachers of English as a foreign language at primary level. She is currently investigating the nature and role of metaphor in children's language and learning.

**Ian Davies** is a lecturer in the Department of Educational Studies at the University of York. His previous experience includes ten years as a teacher in comprehensive schools. His masters and doctoral theses were concerned with political education in schools in England. Recent and forthcoming research and development work include projects on education for European citizenship, teachers' perceptions of models of political learning, and international comparisons of the meaning of citizenship.

**Hilary Emery** was a teacher in primary schools for twelve years before joining Hampshire's Assessment and Records of Achievement team. In 1991 she joined the School Examination and Assessment Council, working on Key Stage 1 assessment and recording achievement in primary and secondary schools. She has since moved to Worcester College of Higher Education to work on initial teacher education and has taken a particular interest in helping students assess and record their development as teachers in the classroom, as well as continuing to work with teachers and children in schools.

**Ken Fox** is a senior lecturer in media education at Christ Church College, Canterbury, Kent. Trained as a primary school teacher, he worked for nine years as a classroom teacher before taking up his current post at Christ Church. He teaches on B.Ed and in-service courses and continues to develop workshop activities in media education with primary and secondary teachers and pupils.

**Pamela Munn** is professor of curriculum research, Moray House Institute of Education, Heriot-Watt University. She has a long-standing research interest in school discipline and related areas such as bullying and truancy. She is currently working on a major research project on school exclusions.

**Joy Palmer** is reader in education, director of the Centre for Research on Environmental Thinking and Awareness and deputy dean of the Faculty of Social Sciences at the University of Durham. She is a vice president of the National Association for Environmental Education and a member of the Commission on Education and Communication of the IUCN (World Conservation Union). She has published extensively in the fields of education and environmental education.

**Graham Vulliamy** is a senior lecturer in the Department of Educational Studies at the University of York and has collaborated with Rosemary Webb in her research on primary education. They have researched the impact of the 1988 Education Reform Act on primary schools in England and Wales and are currently working with Finnish researchers on a comparative study of curriculum change in English and Finnish primary schools.

**Rosemary Webb** lectures in the Department of Educational Studies at the University of York and is currently Chair of the Association for the Study of Primary Education (ASPE). She has taught for over ten years in primary and middle schools and from 1989–91 was professional officer for primary education in the National Curriculum Council.

# Index

SHACKLETON'S WAY

This book is due for return on or before the last date shown below.

SIR ERNEST SHACKLETON, 1874–1922